30-SOMETHING MILLIONAIRE

Mohit Chawla runs his investment office, Bimtek Group, in India: focused on capital markets, real estate, infrastructure and early-stage venture investments.

Mohit comes with around two decades of diverse experience, having worked in the financial markets (both buy and sell side) across Europe, the US, the Middle East and India; and in real estate design, development and consultancy. He is a two-time entrepreneur, having successfully built, scaled and exited venture-capital backed start-ups.

Mohit was an investment banker with Goldman Sachs (Financial Institutions Group, EMEA) and Morgan Stanley Real Estate EMEA London desk, as well as advisor to the world's largest infrastructure private equity: GIP's Asia platform, Equis.

Mohit holds a bachelor's degree from Indian Institute of Technology (IIT) Roorkee, a master's in management, majoring in finance from HEC Paris (graduating with the *Dean's List Roll of Honors*) and a graduate diploma from Stanford University. He's a featured profile in *Forbes'* publication on 'Young Leaders of the Future, 2016'. For his academic excellence, he was felicitated with the 'Charpak' Scholar Award by the French government in 2013 and 2014.

In his leisure time, besides reading, meditating and following sports, Mohit actively contributes to the Indian ecosystem as an advisor, guest lecturer, keynote speaker and business-plan competition judge at premier institutions such as IIT, Delhi University and industry and investo͏ HT Media, GRE Club among oth͏ his association with football for ove at club- and state-level across region

Learn more about Bimtek her͏ Mohit here: https://www.linkedin.com/in/cnawlamohit/.

30 SOMETHING MILLIONAIRE

How NOT to Ace the Rat Race ...
Yet Be Successful & Wealthy

Mohit Chawla

WESTLAND
BUSINESS

WESTLAND
BUSINESS

Published by Westland Business, an imprint of Westland Books, a division of Nasadiya Technologies Private Limited, in 2026

No. 269/2B, First Floor, 'Irai Arul', Vimalraj Street, Nethaji Nagar, Alapakkam Main Road, Maduravoyal, Chennai 600095

Westland, the Westland logo, Westland Business and the Westland Business logo are the trademarks of Nasadiya Technologies Private Limited, or its affiliates.

ISBN: 9789371976084

10 9 8 7 6 5 4 3 2 1

Typeset by Mukul

Printed at Thomson Press India Private Limited

*To Shri Pancham Padshahi ji Gurumaharaj ji, my spiritual guru,
for his gracious guidance towards a broader purpose in life.*

*And my parents: mother, Bimla Chawla and father (Papaji),
Tek Chand Chawla: together the 'Bimtek' of my life.
For I am nothing but a mere reflection of their value system.*

Contents

Part III
Broader Learnings and Purpose of Life

Introduction

Compound interest is the eighth wonder of the world; one who understands it, earns it; one who doesn't, pays it.

—Albert Einstein

THE STORY IS COBBLED TOGETHER FROM THE LIFE OF ANOTHER 'regular' Indian guy who realised, very early on, that what we were taught in school as children was quite contrary to reality. Specifically, the idea that being a 'master of one' is somehow better than being a 'jack of all trades'.

In truth, the power of being a jack of many trades often compounds into magnificence across almost every field of life. We leverage the lessons and experiences from one area into another, each adding up and strengthening the whole. It all connects, it all amplifies.

I was fortunate to grasp very early on how the underlying compound effect works wonders if applied in life. To remind myself of its importance, I even edited my phone wallpapers to carry one message across every screen: 'Consistency, Discipline and Patience—both in personal and professional life.'

If the building blocks are laid correctly and maintained over a long period, they lead to compounding in every sphere—personal well-being, prosperity, wealth, peace of mind and harmony in relationships, society and the larger ecosystem.

The story culminates in these very principles that have guided me well and, I believe, can also serve the reader. Thus, the idea of sharing this journey.

As for me, the author, I am an investor by passion and a 'wannabe' writer. I run an investment office, Bimtek Capital, which rests on two main foundations:

- Simple principles of life, across personal, professional and spiritual dimensions;
- The principles of investment greats such as Ben Graham, Warren Buffett, Peter Lynch and Howard Marks, and leveraging their learnings along with the fundamental principles of value investing to apply them in Indian capital markets.

The idea is not just to generate superior risk-adjusted returns, which have historically sparked awe, but also to live a high-quality life, think independently, leave the conventional rat race and be able to arrive at a stage where money stops being a question, constraint or a limiting factor.

This idea for this book came from this exact thought: how could I possibly assist others to cut through the noise and guide them towards a state of life where comfort, stability and clarity coexist? Where one is comfortable in every sense of the word!

The Japanese concept of ikigai describes this pursuit well. It lies at the intersection of:

1. What one is good at
2. What one is passionate about
3. What one can be paid for, and
4. What the world needs.

Easier said than done, since most people end up living conventional work lives, forever chasing either their 'passion' or what they are good at and would make commercial sense. Simply put, they make a livelihood that sustains them; they rarely do both. Many, if not most, sleepwalk through life, weighed down by challenges and struggles. As Buddhism rightly points out, human life is filled with struggles.

Through my own journey, I discovered that my ikigai lies at the intersection of three things:

a) Attaining financial independence
b) Cultivating mental peace and
c) Creating value—for myself, the people who matter in my life and for the broader ecosystem.

That ecosystem begins with immediate family and friends, extends to the nation and, for some, can even stretch to humanity at large. My skillset in finance and investing from points (a) and (b) cover points 1,2,3 from the ikigai concept mapped above, while (c) aligns naturally with point 4.

Ultimately, life is about weaving together everything we learn—spiritual, personal and professional—while cutting through noise and distractions, for that frees us from trivial issues and channels our energies into things that truly matter: the levers that make an impact, move life meaningfully forward and help fulfil the purpose of our lives.

Setting the Stage

The book is structured in three parts, with a total of fourteen chapters.

Part 1 focuses on personal life learnings—the upbringing, value systems, familial teachings and the all-important foundation that acts as the springboard for everything ahead in life.

In my case, the foundational elements came from my parents' teachings (*sanskaar*), an early embrace of spirituality and meditation and the appreciation of a broader purpose of life through my association with Shri Paramhans Advait Mat and Shri Anandpur. Meditation has since become an integral part of my being, a core practice that has brought equanimity to my life and conduct.

Another crucial part of this foundation was my educational and professional 'launchpad'—my years at Vidyamandir Classes (a coaching institute for the IIT entrance exam, IIT-JEE). The life lessons imparted by its co-founding brothers were invaluable: learning to be self-reliant, to think independently and to develop a problem-solving mindset. These teachings instilled in me a DNA-like trait that has defined my character: the thought process of planning things—chalking out a vision, putting together a strategy to achieve it and thereafter keeping my head down and going at it each day with consistency, discipline and patience. Over time, the *compounding effect* of these habits have made all the difference!

Part 2 covers what I call the 'commercial backbone' of life— the cogwheels of the money-making life machine. This section brings together learnings and key takeaways from education, professional experiences and day-to-day life—all put together in the form of a mindset, a mental checklist and a day-to-day execution framework that readers can apply in their own journeys.

Here, the narrative spans over two-and-a-half decades of my higher education and professional career. We follow the journey across the IIT years: cracking one of the most competitive exams in the world, getting the coveted 'IITian' tag (a 'chip on the shoulder' and a gateway to opportunities across the world basis the network and learnings) and the nuances of my time at the institute.

The story continues through global institutions, Stanford University and HEC Paris School of Management, bringing both contrasts and commonalities in my learning journey across the best of Indian and international institutes.

Professionally, this phase follows the fearless, hungry-to-conquer-the-world mindset of a nineteen-year-old founder juggling higher education along with the challenges of building a business from the ground up. Thereafter, we share the experiences of working with and learning from the best in the world of investment banking and private equity at Goldman Sachs and Morgan Stanley (across London, New York, Dubai) and appreciating the flow of financial capital across the world and the impact at the largest of scale: on nations, economies and global enterprises. The networks and relationships built during these years unlocked doors 'anywhere and everywhere' one wishes to be in life, while also creating the foundation for financial independence with the outrageous monetary benefits that come along with this.

All of this then tied into my entrepreneurial journey 2.0 in India—working towards my own ikigai and building value for the ecosystem. Essentially, this was a move back home to 'Make in India, for the world'.

Part 3 focuses on the principles of life across spiritual, personal and professional spheres. They explore the larger *purpose of life*, framed both philosophically and practically.

This part attempts to answer the timeless questions: Why are we here? What is the purpose of our life? How do we balance spirituality with rationality? It leans on both spiritual and scientific lenses in pursuit of a 'middle path' each of us might find for ourselves.

In my case, I unknowingly followed the Advait Vedanta philosophy and a practice of meditation since childhood. A decade later, through research and reflection, I realised how Advait Vedanta closely aligns with Buddhism, and is one of the rare equanimous philosophical paths, balancing spirituality with rationality and scientific inquiry. It also reaffirmed my belief that life often has its own plan for each of us—whether we call it karma, fate, divine will or simply the universe transpiring to materialise our manifestations.

Here, I draw lessons by questioning, experiencing and engaging with schools of thought across science, faith and spirituality. Along the way, we stand 'on the shoulders of giants', learning from the wisdom of some of the world's most accomplished individuals across fields.

The goal is to assemble a framework of building blocks that anyone can use to achieve personal peace, professional success, financial freedom and, ultimately, a sense of life's higher purpose.

These are the very building blocks that have shaped me into who I am and in getting to where I am in life today—the 'principles of life' that I believe can benefit anyone, anywhere, if practised with consistency.

A Note to the Reader

Throughout the chapters, I have flagged the 'Life Lessons' that have served me well—presented as 'Guiding Principles' worth reflecting on and, wherever helpful, adopting into your own life.

If you prefer to skip around, the headers and life lessons (in bold) are designed to help you dive in and out. That said, I strongly recommend reading Chapters 10 to 14 in sequence. These passages distil the essential learnings compiled here—drawing from the wisdom of celebrated people across industries as well as the 'low-hanging fruits' of life across personal, professional and spiritual domains. These closing chapters embody the central purpose of this book.

My hope is to assist readers in navigating their own life trajectory, wherever they may be in their journey, since these learnings apply across ages and stages—and if they can add even a little clarity, direction or peace to your path, my purpose in writing this book should have been served well.

Here's hoping you enjoy reading this as much as I enjoyed writing it, and that you take away something valuable with you from this book.

Happy reading!

Part I

Personal Life

1

Early Years

Familial Upbringing, Wisdom and Value System: Sanskaar

Born in a North Indian family in New Delhi, the capital of India, I had a childhood typical of Indian households back in the day, i.e., a joint-family set-up, with my dad and two of his brothers with their respective families—their wives and kids—living in the same house on different floors, with our grandparents living on the ground floor of the house.

Three of my father's younger brothers lived in a similar way on different floors in another house close to ours, and his four sisters were married and living with their families. In case you were wondering—yes, this was a big joint family.

I had been 'blessed' with five uncles and four aunts, my father being the third of ten children. The concept of nuclear families came into wide practice a few decades later, in the late 1990s or early 2000s. For most of the post-Independence period, the Indian government encouraged families to have children to grow the population, to the extent that the government rewarded people with land parcels for having a dozen kids. There are 1.4 billion of us around the world now. In all sanity, the policy is not prevalent anymore!

Adverse circumstances and tragedy are the epicentre of innovation and success. I learnt this personally from my family tree. There's a saying in India that goes: *'The first generation earns, the second compounds and the third ruins it.'* A similar saying in the Western world is: *'The first generation sows, the second generation grows and the third generation blows.'*

My grandfather and his siblings were the third generation and a living validation of the above wisdom. I still see the shine in my dad's eyes whenever he recalls the story about the business set-up and run by my great-great-grandfather—the family used to be one of the major producers of ice cream in India back in my father's childhood. A feud in my grandfather's generation and some of the misdeeds of the siblings eventually took the business down to the ground.

My father was only sixteen when this happened. Seeing my grandfather in a near-shocked state of mind, going from riches to rags, my father quit his studies while in the tenth grade and requested my grandfather to quasi-retire from work. He insisted that his two elder brothers, who were both studying engineering at that time, continue with their studies, and that he would quit school to work and provide for the family as well as pay for his elder brothers' engineering studies along with the younger siblings' education.

His first day of work was as a tea stall vendor—he set up a roadside tea shop at a bus station in Garhmukhteshwar, in the state of Uttar Pradesh in North India, the place which hosts one of the largest festivals in India, Kumbh. As luck would have it, he sold out within a few hours on his first day. A few weeks in, he rented a shop and started a proper tea shop selling tea, cookies and some other Indian snacks near the same bus station. Soon enough, by God's grace, the business picked up to the level where he scaled up to a sweet shop, selling traditional Indian sweets along with tea and other refreshments.

Business had become so good that his shop would sell out each day within a few hours of opening. Some of the nearby shopkeepers grew jealous of him and would try to hamper his business by shooing away the customers and even attempting to beat him up. A bit of strong-arming was prevalent in some of the northern states of India such as UP and Bihar—it still is. But as the saying goes in India, *Bhole ka Bhagwan* (God takes care of the innocent). My father tells me how he would keep chanting 'Bhagwan ji, Bhagwan ji' all day long in his heart while at work, and how everything would take care of itself.

Two points of clarification before we move ahead: first, my father is the single biggest inspiration in my life and thus this section is dedicated to him and to the sanskaars (values) that I have imbibed from him. Second, we shall be leveraging a few Indian anecdotal, albeit cultural, references across the book, and I will try to explain them as we go along.

Besides taking care of the family, my father provided for the higher education of his two elder brothers, both civil engineers, and thus laid the groundwork for the family's eventual real estate business. One brother went on to become the chief engineer with the Municipal Corporation of Delhi, and the other, after practising as an engineer for over thirty years, moved to academia and now serves as a professor of civil engineering at an eminent private university in India.

My father has been the anchor of the family, fulfilling his duties as a son, brother and family man; taking care of all the siblings' education and weddings and helping them create a launch pad for their professional lives too. I can't imagine the determination of a sixteen-year-old—to take everything upon himself, provide for everyone, set aside his aspirations of studying or working on a career for himself and start from scratch.

Although he missed out on a formal education, through his experiences later in life, he became a self-taught civil engineer. Through the years, his passion and drive have been to ensure his kids get what he could not: the best of education.

Foundation: Early Learning from the Master Himself

I think a few of us realise late in life how lucky we are to be born into the right family, to the right parents and in the right familial setup. Be it our karma, God's grace or just pure luck, appreciating this is the starting point of my story.

I didn't recognise it soon enough—how simply watching my father conduct himself through the years would serve as one of the biggest learnings in my life.

While his brothers practised as civil engineers, my father began working as an independent contractor for civil, infrastructure and real-estate projects across Delhi. With his team, he helped build a major share of Delhi's infrastructure as it exists today—roads, parks, sewage systems—as well as social infrastructure such as schools, swimming pools and gymnasiums.

He then went on to start his own real estate venture—a quasi-private equity outfit at a small scale—where he would buy land, develop it for residential or commercial use and either sell it or hold it as a rental-yielding asset. It was consistent with the simple, tried-and-tested model of real estate private equity: 'Buy it, fix it, sell it.'

Over time, he built and managed a real estate business portfolio using his own 'standard operating procedures' which, in hindsight, mirrored the structure of investment committees of some of the largest real estate funds, and consistent with the principles taught by great investors in their classic books.

I have been fortunate to observe all this in real life and learn naturally from him. These early lessons laid the foundation for my study as an architect and civil engineer. They also shaped my career in real estate, often setting me apart from colleagues in different environments, thanks to practical, on-ground knowledge and the head start it gave me.

From starting at a tea stall, to setting up a sweet shop, to working as a civil contractor for the Municipal Corporation of Delhi, becoming a Class-1 (highest-graded) contractor and eventually building his own real estate business—the story has been nothing short of inspirational!

———◆———

Besides other inheritances, I feel I have been fortunate with a great value system from my father—his brains, his skills and his values—or what one might call the modern-day 'Shravan Kumar' concept, i.e., treating your parents as God figures and recognising how, with their blessings, the world conspires to provide for everything one could ever imagine, or even things one might not have aspired to.

I'll explain.

Despite my father providing for and helping set up the careers and lives of his siblings, all of them eventually moved ahead with their own lives, as the family branched out from being a joint family to smaller nuclear families. Over time, his siblings distanced themselves from my grandparents.

I saw my father take care of his parents in their final years, while his siblings weren't interested in even checking on them, let alone taking care of them. My grandparents, teary-eyed at times, would bless him with both hands on his head.

One incident comes to mind: at one point, my grandmother wasn't keeping well and had to be hospitalised for a few days. During this time, one of my maternal aunt's daughters was getting married, and my parents, along with us kids, travelled to attend the wedding in Karnal, Haryana.

Back at the hospital, the doctors told the family that my grandmother was doing better and could be discharged that very day. Funnily enough, due to a local mob issue, the Haryana government sealed its borders with Delhi for two days and did not allow people to travel across. Because of this, we were stuck there and unable to return home.

To our surprise, when we got back to Delhi two days later, we learnt that none of my father's siblings had gone to the hospital to get their mother (my grandmother) discharged. And why? The hospital bill was around 400,000 rupees (~$5,000), and none of them wanted to pay it.

I still remember how my grandparents were teary-eyed when we finally went to the hospital to bring them home. They blessed my father, saying, *'Bhagwan tujhe khoob rang lagaega, bete! Tu soch bhi nahi sakta kitni tarakki karega tu.'* ('God will grace you with immeasurable success, son! You can't even imagine how far you'll go.')

Such has been his dedication on the personal front.

Professionally, I have seen my father work harder than most—if not all—people I've met in my life. And I say this after having had the privilege of working across geographies with some of the best and sharpest minds in the world.

His commitment to work and his responsibilities was such that, as a child, I hardly ever got to see him. I would wake up in the morning and he would already be gone for work by 6 or 7 a.m., and by the time he returned home around midnight or 1 a.m., I would be fast asleep. My mother would sometimes tell me how my father kissed me on the forehead before leaving for work, and again when he came home late at night, simply because he couldn't spend proper time with me.

This continued for a good six to seven years during my childhood. Not that his working hours changed very much later, but by then I had started waking up early to play football before school, or staying up late just to spend a little time with him.

Some of us fancy investment bankers across London, New York and other financial hubs of the world show off and gather sympathy for how our overpaid jobs 'kill' us with 16–18-hour days and nearly 90–100-hour weeks. But little did I know back then that my father, and countless other successful people, had quietly worked just as hard, sacrificing their personal lives in order to *build* something!

There's a saying in Hindi, *'Bin mare swarg nahi hai.'* (Literally: You cannot go to heaven without dying first.) The essence of it is that hard work eventually pays off. One may not appreciate or see the results in the short term, but over the medium to long term, it pays off, sometimes even through sheer luck. This was a lesson I witnessed early on, and it has stayed with me ever since.

The value system I picked up from my parents has been pivotal, not just in my personal life, but also in the way I conduct myself professionally.

> **Life Lesson #1:** Learning from parents is the best education, and their blessings make the world around us fall into place in ways we could never imagine.
>
> **Life Lesson #2:** God resides within us—in our hearts—and physically in the form of our parents. The sooner we realise this, the better our lives turn out to be.

2

Spirituality and Meditation

Paramhans Dayalji and Shri Anandpur

I BELIEVE MYSELF TO BE A MAN OF SCIENCE, ALBEIT THERE ARE softer aspects and sometimes even incidents in life which make you realise that there is a higher power that has a plan for you. As the celebrated trance music band Swedish House Mafia sings in one of their tracks, *'Don't you worry, don't you worry, child! See heaven's got a plan for you.'* Or, as the Bhagavad Gita advises: focus on doing your work without expecting results or favourable outcomes.

Sometimes, being in the right place at the right time, or being introduced to something, is all destiny—or maybe God's way of taking care of us. Since childhood, as a twelve-year-old, I have been associated with Shri Anandpur: an Indian spiritual society guiding people on how one could channel their energies and live life in pursuit of the true purpose of human existence—self-realisation and unification of our soul with the higher soul (or God soul)—while living one's day-to-day life as usual.

Essentially, this is the basis of the Advait Vedanta school of Indian philosophy. Shri Anandpur was founded by Shri Paramhans Dayalji, who was a proponent of Advait Vedanta philosophy.

The background to this story is that, around the time I was ten, my family lost both my grandmother and one of my uncles (my father's younger brother) on the same day. My uncle had just cleared the selection test for the Indian Civil Services, but one night while studying, he suffered a severe asthma attack. He was rushed to the emergency room of a nearby hospital, where he was accidentally injected with a dose of an incorrect medicine and died on the spot. My grandmother, who had not been keeping well, died of shock a few hours later.

I was very young when this happened, but I saw a major change in my father from then on. He began questioning life and its purpose, and this deepened his inclination towards spirituality, both through Anandpur and through the broader concept of giving back to society. He has been a spiritual man all his life. My parents' home has a pooja (prayer) room where they perform aarti (prayers) every day, twice a day, morning and evening. After my grandparents passed away, my father even built a temple in Delhi in their remembrance, installing a bust of my grandparents there. He does numerous other things in terms of giving back to society, and he doesn't like to talk about them since he's the conventional old-school kind of man, who believes in doing things and not talking about them. I couldn't agree more.

I feel blessed to have been associated with Shri Anandpur through my parents. Over time, I have picked up lessons and habits from this association that have stayed with me and helped define my character.

The Bhagavad Gita lays out nine principles that a person should follow on the path to enlightenment and liberation. Shri Anandpur's five 'guiding principles' for daily practice are consistent with these. They are: *Shri Aarti Puja* (prayer), *Seva* (selfless service, giving back), *Simran* (meditation), *Satsang* (learning and knowledge through spiritual discussions or readings) and *Dhyaan* (the realisation that we are one with the God soul—non-dualism—and cultivating equanimity in conduct).

As Shri Paramhans Dayalji would often say:

Shri Aarti Pooja, Seva, Simran, Satsang aur Dhyaan
Shraddha sahit nit sevan karo, nishchay ho kalyan.

Should one follow these five principles daily, success is bound to follow in every aspect of life.

Shri Paramhans Dayalji founded Shri Anandpur Trust in the nineteenth century, along with Shri Anandpur Ashram—a 12,000-acre spiritual settlement in Madhya Pradesh, India. Legend has it that the land where Anandpur stands was originally barren. The Scindia royal family of Madhya Pradesh had declared that whoever could establish a self-sustaining ecosystem on that barren land would be awarded the land itself as a prize.

Many individuals and communities tried and failed. But by the grace of Shri Paramhans Dayalji, Anandpur gradually evolved from a barren wasteland into a thriving ecosystem. Today, everything required for life is self-produced within its 12,000 acres—food, agricultural produce, infrastructure, education, even energy. The only thing sourced from outside is salt, since one can't produce salt on land.

At Anandpur, you can see fertile agricultural fields, charitable hospitals, schools providing free education, renewable electricity production, infrastructure and amenities, along with spiritual places of worship. The residents—all members who live there full time—have devoted their lives to service. They conduct day-to-day life with simplicity, dedicating themselves to helping others fulfil their life purpose and serving as examples for others on the path to enlightenment.

The peace and tranquillity of Anandpur are indescribable. The very air carries calmness. Everyone there is immersed in *seva* (service) allocated to them, with utmost dedication, whether distributing food in the *langar* hall, doing cleaning and maintenance or any other act of service—along with practising the five guiding principles. It is the one place in the world, besides home, where my heart truly finds peace. It's the place where I would want to be buried. The literal sense of rest in peace.

I cannot describe in words the blessings of Shri Paramhans Dayalji and how his presence has guided me in life. It feels like a constant light that makes me believe I can accomplish anything I set out to. Such is the grace of the higher power guiding our lives.

Possibly a Proof of Higher Power (God Soul)?

I had learnt while studying physics in high school that, scientifically, it has been proven that had the force of gravity been higher than what it is, the universe would likely have imploded into the size of a handball. On the other hand, had it been any lower, the universe would likely have exploded. Further, the ratio of electromagnetic force to gravitational force is 1 per cent, precisely enough for life to sustain on Earth.

There are certain atmospheres where we may be able to amend semantics and explore habitability, albeit the precise nature of these scientific facts—and thus the sustenance of life on Earth—point to the likelihood of a creator, a higher power (or God soul).

Thus, my personal view and inclination are towards the middle path of rationality: being a man of both science and religion, instead of *science versus religion*, as most of us tend to interpret it. Or, as German philosopher Immanuel Kant famously said: '*I had to deny knowledge in order to make room for faith.*'

He was not suggesting the outright rejection of knowledge, but rather that he believed true objective knowledge is limited, and that one can only know what is perceived through the senses and understood through reason.

The Underlying Principle and Learnings from Meditation

I feel blessed to have had this human life where my mind is spiritually aligned and possibly on the path to awakening with meditation, the inherent peace at my core and the desire to fulfil the purpose of my human life—whether for my own soul and physical self, my family and friends, or society at large. This is what keeps me content and happy—the real source of grateful bliss.

I started meditating at the age of twelve, when I was introduced to Paramhans Dayalji and Shri Anandpur through my parents. Ever since, I follow the five 'guiding principles' of Shri Anandpur on a daily basis. Simran (meditation) is one of them—it is practised through Pranayama, a form of meditation where one focuses on breathing. I focus on the *Shiv Netra* spot on my forehead (the 'third eye' spot as it is often called) along with my breathing. Over time, the focus shifts higher—above the forehead and eventually towards the head—where one starts to realise and experience the cosmos and the microcosmic world in its true essence, i.e., the genesis that we reside in the world and the microcosmic world resides in us.

Meditation is believed to be a means to this path of enlightenment. Gautam Buddha experienced and preached this on the basis of his own learnings, as do some, if not most, of the other spiritual schools of thought across the world.

Since childhood, meditation has become an integral part of my life, to the extent that it feels as basic as eating each day. It was instrumental during my two years of preparation for the Indian Institute of Technology Joint Entrance Exam, better known as IIT-JEE.

I would wake up at 4 a.m., meditate for half an hour, and then study with utmost concentration for three hours before rushing to school by 8 a.m. For such competitive examinations, most kids would study and slog for ten to twelve hours each day for over two years. Yet there I was, doing three hours of self-study in the morning and a couple of hours in the evening, and still felt on top of things. No, I am not a genius. The deeper concentration that came from meditation was the difference. No secret! I would truly implore you to give it a try.

Meditation, and by extension the equanimity it brings—a balanced and centred state of mind—is bliss. It not only increases one's concentration but also feels like the cheat code to Daniel Kahneman's *Thinking, Fast and Slow*, wherein, instead of reacting to situations, the 'slow' part of the brain starts operating in a way that brings greater clarity and enables rational decision-making. This increases the odds of being right and, by extension, the odds of success.

> **Life Lesson #3:** Realising our purpose in life and the role of spirituality in attaining it.

The blend of sanskaars from my family and my association with Shri Anandpur became pivotal pillars in the early years of my life. Little did I know that the learnings from Shri Anandpur—about questioning, and thereby seeking to understand the purpose of one's life and then acting accordingly to attain that and to be on the path to self-realisation—would make me more aware and awakened in life, and play a pivotal role every single day thereafter, both personally and professionally.

3

Vidyamandir and IIT: Keechad me Kamal

Vidyamandir Classes: A Springboard for Independent Thinking

THE INDIAN INSTITUTES OF TECHNOLOGY (IITs) ARE A GROUP of seven premier campuses across India that have produced some of the country's most celebrated achievers. The prestige and fandom they command in India is star-like. Parents aspire for their children to attend an IIT, study at the best engineering institutions and graduate with highly coveted, well-paying jobs, sometimes with salaries running into eight figures in Indian rupees, earning the 'crorepati' tag.

The glorification runs so high that books have been written and movies made about the IITs, making a few writers, filmmakers and actors famous by extension. The obsession goes so far that websites and platforms exist to facilitate matchmaking for IITians—and shockingly, even seek dowries—based on these 'fancy' degrees. The competition to get in is intense, to say the least.

Until tenth grade in the Indian education system (equivalent to US high school or UK A-Levels), I was a pretty average student. I typically scored in the high 70s or low 80s overall each year, while also engaging in extracurricular activities—playing football, taking part in the dramatics society, singing and serving in the Bharat Scouts & Guides, the civilian equivalent of military services in India. I had *no idea* what IITs were, or of their grandeur!

It was only in the tenth grade, during my board exams, that I scored 96.6 per cent overall and realised that I could be good at academics too. After the results, students were discussing their streams for higher education: medical, non-medical (engineering), commerce or arts: the four specialisation options available for eleventh- and twelfth-graders at the time.

That was when I first heard about IITs from a friend, and also learnt that to realistically make it there, one needed to join a coaching institute. For me, that was Vidyamandir Classes (VMC), at the time a Delhi-based institute (now pan-India) with one of the highest success rates. Roughly 90–95 per cent of VMC students cleared IIT-JEE, compared with the national odds of 0.2 per cent—as over a million candidates competed for only 2,000–3,000 spots across the seven IITs.

'*Lakhon mein ek!*' (One in a million), as the saying goes.

Over the years, the number of IIT campuses and available seats has expanded, and many other coaching institutions have sprung up. Some cities in India—like Kota, Rajasthan—have even centred their economies around IIT coaching. But in Delhi back then, VMC was *the* place to be for IIT aspirants.

Learning about the IITs and VMC, I also realised something about myself and human nature: we're often driven to do what others aspire to and to be better than them. This is the foundation of a competitive mindset, the instinct to win the rat race. This is the mindset one seeks to leave behind, following the takeaways discussed subsequently in this book.

That dreaded summer afternoon in May when I took the VMC entrance exam still gives me chills when I recall it. Think of a student who has just scored 96.6 per cent in high school—one of the top results in my school, Delhi, and even the country that year—now sitting down for a three-hour test. Within the first fifteen minutes, I realised I had no idea how to solve even one of the six questions asked!

Having read the first question and unable to make sense of even a word of what was asked, I skipped to the second. Realising the same for the second question, I told myself that maybe I was having an off day and should turn the question paper around, start from the back and attempt the last question first. Failing to make sense of the last question and subsequently the other three as well, my heart sank: the first 15 minutes of the exam were up, and I hadn't written a word on the answer sheet besides my name and enrolment number! I looked around the room in bewilderment, wondering whether I was the dumb one or whether everyone else was equally lost.

As you will appreciate, examination rooms are supposed to be quiet with ample lighting and fresh air for the test-takers to sit and write their answers in peace. The exam hall was silent, but not in the usual way—it was a tense, ghastly kind of silence, like those few moments after one experiences a shock. Since I had ample time to do almost nothing, I excused myself to the washroom, splashed water on my face, looked in the mirror and reminded myself that things couldn't get any worse and that I might as well go back in and try to solve at least one question that I could make some sense of.

I went back in to attempt the question I understood best. By the end of three hours, I had managed two-and-a-half questions out of six. When the results came, I had scored 19 out of 100, probably my lowest academic score ever. But astonishingly, I was selected as 1 of just 200 students out of the 5,000–6,000 who had taken the test. That was my entry into Vidyamandir Classes to prepare for the IIT entrance examination over the course of the next two years.

> **Life Lesson #4:** Relative performance matters in the world, NOT just absolute performance. *Thus, the importance of giving your best and NOT giving up, no matter what!*

This humbling experience taught me the importance of persistence. Though I knew little in that exam, I still got through—because I sat through, tried to solve whatever I could and refused to give up. Obviously, it also made me appreciate the fact that if I were to crack the actual entrance exam for the IITs, I had my task cut out for me.

Splashing water on the face when one is almost down and out, akin to the habit of having coffee when one is near sleepy, has stayed with me till date—when I just get up in the middle of work or whatever I am up to and step away, when feeling low, to splash water on my face and remind myself of that dreaded Vidyamandir entrance examination and how I got through that. So, this (any current problem) situation too shall pass!

The next two years revealed to me, for the first time, the compound effect of consistency, discipline and patience. Unlike most other institutes where students slogged twelve to sixteen hours a day in marathon schedules including lectures each day, Vidyamandir followed a completely different model. We had only one three-hour lecture per week. Each Sunday lecture covered one topic—physics, chemistry or mathematics—taught by one of the three brothers who founded VMC (all IIT alumni). A week before each lecture, we received notes, reference material and problem sets with clear instructions to self-study thoroughly before the class. Essentially, the idea was to come for the session as if it were a dedicated exam for that particular topic and not a study session.

During the lecture, we would learn much more about the particular topic as well as the relevant problems. This would not just deepen our understanding of the concept but also allow us to appreciate our self-study done pre-lecture even more, as the concepts were baked in further. The following week was spent cold-towelling through the concepts from this lecture, re-attempting the problem sets, clearly setting the subject topic in our head and heart, and thereafter preparing for the next lecture in the same way.

Contrast this with thousands of other students cramming formulas and memorising theories for hours each day, overlaid with lectures: essentially a pink sauce pasta of fourteen to sixteen hours of study. Our looped weekly process: consistently cutting through the noise of what's happening around, doing the simple and boring routine of focusing on one thing at a time, delving deeper into it by our own selves and using the teaching faculty's guidance in the three-hour session to hit the nail on the head and clear the specific subject concept in our heads, essentially made us *self-reliant* and *independent thinkers*. These are two of the most under-talked but necessary skills observed in highly successful people across domains in the world.

During those two years of preparation, my routine became rigorous but balanced: waking at 4 a.m., meditating for half an hour, three peaceful hours of self-study and thereafter rush to reach school by 8 a.m. (almost always late!) and spend six hours across lectures, time with friends, playing football, enjoying music or engaging in other extracurricular activities such as dramatics, Bharat (India) Scouts and Guides. I would then come back home around 2–3 p.m., eat, relax, nap and rest for a few hours and put in another 2–3-hour self-study session before going to bed early and repeating the process.

I would learn from other kids at school how they were up till 3–4 a.m. at night, studying ten to twelve hours at a stretch after school, then being half-asleep during the day, going through the motions and sitting through lectures at school and returning home to another day of the same (almost dreaded!) twelve-hour process. Thinking about this almost negative feedback cycle gives me chills!

I still fondly remember struggling with I.E. Irodov's *Problems in General Physics*. Just a single one to two–liner, innocent-seeming problem from that book would keep me scratching my head for hours as I struggled to solve it, but it taught me the important lesson of sticking through problems, no matter long it takes and applying myself without giving up.

In the end, 195 of the 200 students from our batch made it to the IITs—a staggering 95 per cent success rate, and nearly 1 in 10 of the ~2,500 students admitted nationwide that year.

Looking back, those two years formed one of the most important phases of my life. I learnt to be self-reliant, a self-starter, think independently and have consistency and discipline in my life to witness first-hand the magic of compounding that leads to success!

Life Lesson #5: Declutter. Cut through the noise. Focus on building your skill set, showing up and giving your best each day. Trust the process. Even if it feels repetitive or boring, consistency compounds into success. Most people give up somehow, somewhere. Don't!

Learnings and Un-learnings at IIT

The time spent at IIT helped me become a better human being: less of an engineer or practising architect and more of an evolved person with a balanced personality, aware of the intricacies of the Indian ecosystem and life at large.

The softer learnings came from the social and cultural diversity, and from spending time with peers from different parts and socioeconomic strata of India. I came to appreciate the hustle and struggles of those who came from the smallest, remotest villages and still made it into the country's premier institutions.

The chairman of Infosys, a major information technology services company based out of India, Narayana Murthy, once said that he couldn't buy an admission seat for his son at an IIT, even if he wanted to. This illustrates how IITs truly level the playing field for students, regardless of background, who are willing to put in the effort to create a better life for themselves.

On one end, there were kids who came from nothing, such as street food cart operators' children and farmers' kids, alongside the other end of the spectrum—heirs of millionaires and future billionaires. In between them was the majority of us: the Indian middle class. All of us had come to IIT purely on merit. Nothing more, nothing less.

To my mind, education is a great leveller in a society full of differences, and the IITs are the launchpad for those diligent enough to reach for their dreams. That's why an IIT degree becomes a lifelong 'chip on the shoulder', something that opens doors globally on the strength of the network alone. It provides a safety-net or fall-back option of being able to work on a plan B if plan A doesn't work out. It provides the comfort of having a plan B, since having the degree allows you to land a sensible job any day.

The campuses of all IITs are sprawling, lush green, spread across hundreds of acres, with dedicated academic departments, decent (if not world-class) infrastructure and recreational spaces such as clubs, sports grounds and cafés. IIT Roorkee, located about 200 km from Delhi, is one of them.

Besides lecture halls and hostel rooms, I probably spent the most time at IIT Roorkee's cafeteria, Alpahar, and not at the library! In the middle of the open courtyard stood a 200-year-old banyan tree, covering wooden benches with shade. These benches were always buzzing with students—sipping chai, smoking (*sutta*), munching on bun-samosas (the Mumbai *vada pav* equivalent) or having 'Chapo'. The word, an informal acronym for chai-pakoda (tea and fritters), referred to seniors taking juniors out for food, drinks or anything, often just to strengthen bonds.

A typical day began at 8 a.m. with six to eight hours of lectures in the monumental halls of the Civil Engineering and Architecture Department, ending at around 4–5 p.m. Evenings meant hanging out at Alpahar or the Nescafé coffee shop ('Neski'), playing sports, engaging in extracurricular activities across various clubs. Nights meant a mix of ragging sessions (hush hush: still ongoing, though officially banned), copying assignments, weekend trips to Haridwar, Dehradun, Rishikesh and, of course, plenty of banter, booze and substance for some.

Besides the lifelong friendships forged with the 'daru-sutta' gang (yes, our boys' gang was called that for obvious reasons!

I did not engage in the named activities, but was and still am an integral part of this group), some memories stand out: my first management experience—coordinating our college festival *Thomso* with a ten-member team and a budget of ~₹1 crore; a summer internship in Germany and backpacking with friends across Europe, as a nineteen-year-old kid on internship stipend, making the most of the student discount on the three-month Eurail pass by exploring a different country every week (we would take the Friday night train to a city, spend the weekend there, then take the Sunday night Eurail back to the home city, and then repeat!); working on my graduation thesis under some of India's best architects; finding time for an entrepreneurial side hustle; and eventually, discovering the path towards an MBA and a career in finance.

Looking back, these experiences all link back to the value of the IIT network. For instance, the process of applying to business schools usually takes twelve to eighteen months: prepping for GMAT (Graduate Management Aptitude Test i.e., the entrance exam prerequisite for management courses or business school admissions across the world), researching and shortlisting the dream school and others target schools to apply to, writing essays, refining CVs, preparing for interviews and thereafter the final admit/rejection decision. But for me, it was compressed to three or four months. How? Thanks to the IIT network!

We 'lucky' folks were guided by seniors and super-seniors already studying at the world's top B-schools or the alumni from these schools who were now working in the best jobs globally. Over casual conversations at chai-sutta addas or hostel canteens, they shared tips for GMAT prep, application essays, interviews and gave us free access to their study material, CVs and templates. All this, which others might spend almost a year figuring out, we gained over a few conversations, devising a plan of action to ace the process and executing it swiftly over the course of a few months.

In hindsight, the IIT network is invaluable. Networks normalise and compound over time, adding to one's hard work like a multiplier effect. At the risk of sounding arrogant, I paraphrase what I said almost a decade ago in a Forbes interview: 'You realise the effect of where you've been (to study or work) based on the people you are connected to (your network) and the value they add to your life on an ongoing basis.' Another critical takeaway from IIT was the ability to perform under pressure. The curriculum at IIT is not so intense, or so I think, but all through each semester every year, one engages in various activities, so that towards the end of the semester, most if not all students go sleep-deprived for days before and during the final examinations. These exams of all six or seven subjects being taught in a semester are conducted back-to-back over a period of two or three days. Little did I know then how invaluable this skill would turn out to be in my investment banking career later.

Investment banking is arguably one of the highest paying jobs in the world. The prized Goldman Sachs and Morgan Stanley and top investment banking roles across financial centres of the world such as London, New York, Paris, Dubai, etc., are enviable, but they require one to go through the grind of 14–16-hour work days or 90–100-hour work weeks for most of the junior banking years. Even at senior levels, partners and MDs spend 10–12-hour days at work or in meetings and are expected to be available almost 24x7 for business activities. The trade-off is the pay: from hundreds of thousands of dollars at the analyst level to multi-millions at the top, comparable to CXO salaries in global companies. My IIT experience of thriving under pressure directly as well as other soft skills picked up gave me an edge in such environments.

The lessons from one domain often flow into others, creating cross-synergies. That's why I call myself a 'jack of most trades', not a master of one. The learnings from my four years at IIT extended far beyond academics—shaping my personality, resilience and ability to adapt and thrive under any circumstance. From sleeping on wooden planks (*phatta*) with a thin mattress, to navigating campus politics, vices and constant stress, developing multi-tasking skills, the learnings were immense.

One under-appreciated gift of IIT is exposure: access to some of the best and brightest minds across diverse fields. Whether in core engineering, business, management or other paths, this ecosystem surrounds you with mentors, peers and friends who guide you towards the most optimal routes in achieving your goals.

There's a lot written about IITs and the so-called 'IITians', but there's limited first-hand intel out there. Essentially, there aren't many people from IITs talking about it. One of my friends from IIT Roorkee, Ashutosh Dutta, who is now a civil servant, recently wrote a book called *You Should Never Quit*, which is one of the very few books about IIT written by an IITian.

To my mind, this access to talent, industry, subject matter experts and, above all, the communal spirit of helping one another is the true value system of IITs. It stays with us for life, opening doors wherever we go.

I recall being an eighteen-year-old, just days away from leaving for IIT Roorkee, when I sat at home with my father and uncle. They gave me advice that has stayed with me to this day. My uncle warned that people can be spiteful, and the worst way to hurt someone is by trying to mislead their children—since, for most Indian parents, their children's happiness, character and success are their deepest pride.

Coming from a protected North Indian Punjabi household, I hadn't yet been exposed to the diversity of attitudes, lifestyles and value systems that IIT was about to throw me into. But their words stayed: *'Keechad mein kamal'* (the lotus grows from muddy waters) or the saying, *'Where there's muck, there's brass!'* has stayed with me. Despite the dark sides—substance abuse, vices, distractions—I focused on the task at hand, going through the grind and learning to come out stronger, better and hopefully successful. It was my guiding light, powered by my parents' sanskaars and their blessings.

There's a reason we have a saying in India: *'Bade buzurg kaha karte the …'* (Our elders used to say …). As kids, we ignored the learnings, lessons and advice from our parents, thinking they were just lecturing us. But later in life, we realise their words of wisdom were deeply true and that embracing them makes life much easier.

It's like reading: we rarely meet a successful person who doesn't read, because reading is learning from those who came before us—standing on the shoulders of giants. Elders' advice is the same: accumulated experience, tested wisdom, handed down for our benefit. They may not always dress it up in appealing ways, but it comes from love, care and lived experience.

Life Lesson #6: No matter how absurd it may sound in the moment, your parents' advice is the low-hanging fruit of worldly wisdom on the path to success.

Part II

Professional Endeavours

4

Operations Is the Key to Success

'Ideas are worth (almost) nothing. Execution is the key.'

Given the age that we live in—of social media, information and content—it's little to no surprise that there are a lot of people with ideas to work on, and with dreams and aspirations around them.

Not that there weren't people with aspirations and dreams earlier; just that the world is much more interconnected now than it used to be decades ago. People across the world now have access to, and are acquainted with, events everywhere in almost real time.

It's like whenever we notice someone or some business breaking the glass ceiling by filling a gap in an industry, changing its course or having a broader impact, we end up admiring their success, at times even envying how they are doing something which we feel we could also have 'easily' done. In hindsight, the innovation seems blindly obvious, so we think that we could have done it too.

> **Life Lesson #7:** Ideating is the easy part. Executing is the key.

There are countless lectures and lessons on operational excellence and execution frameworks taught in business schools and across the internet. For instance, B-school material defines an *operational excellence framework* as: a set of guidelines designed to help organisations and people achieve operational excellence. The framework's four pillars are: *strategy development, performance management, leadership and culture and process excellence.*

> **Life Lesson #8:** If you cannot see it, likely you cannot do it.

Virat Kohli, ex-captain of the Indian cricket team and arguably one of the best batsmen in the history of the game, has spoken in interviews about a difficult period in 2012–14 when he struggled in both red and white-ball cricket overseas in SENA countries (South Africa, England, New Zealand and Australia). This was the early phase of his cricketing career, when he had already been hailed as the next big thing in world cricket. Despite immense success in Indian subcontinent conditions, some experts began questioning his ability overseas, where celebrated bowlers like James Anderson, Dale Steyn, Mitchell Starc and Trent Boult dominated him.

After returning from an unsuccessful England series in 2013, where he barely scored any runs, Virat went back to the drawing board to identify his weaknesses. And thereafter, he worked on these with his coaches and trained relentlessly to refine his technique. He often spoke about how he would visualise scoring runs against the best bowlers in their home conditions.

With grit, determination, an improved skillset and vision, he transformed himself. Over the next three or five years, he began scoring centuries almost at will, earning the nickname 'King Kohli' and recognition as one of the best to have ever played the game.

The process was simple yet profound: from ideation, to devising a plan, to executing it with consistency, discipline and patience—that's where the magic happened for him, and where it does for all of us.

Life Lesson #9: Having a regret-minimisation framework.

Some may argue that success often lies beyond our control and that luck plays its part. But the fact remains: fortune usually favours those who consistently put in the effort.

Just as many people live by '*you only live once*' (YOLO, in Gen-Z lingo), I have long tried to follow another principle: the *regret minimisation framework*. Simply put, I strive to give my best—100 per cent of my capabilities—be it across personal life or relationships, professional work and across everything. The fundamental idea is: the knowledge, acceptance, and realisation in the heart that we gave our best leaves us in an equanimous state of mind. At the end of the day, we are content that we operated on a 'best effort basis'.

If the outcome is favourable, it makes us happy. If it isn't, then we are not broken—because it becomes a learning experience. There is peace within, knowing we did all we could, and minimal (if any) regret that things might have been different had we tried harder. Essentially, it's about focusing on the process and journey, regardless of the outcome.

As noted in the Bhagavad Gita: If outcomes align with our desires, that is God's grace. If they don't, then it is part of God's larger—and likely better—plan.

The famous poet Harivansh Rai Bachchan echoed the same sentiment in his work: *'Mann ka ho toh achha; na ho toh aur bhi accha.'*

Crème-de-la-Crème: HEC Paris and Start-up with B-school

While studying the concepts of civil engineering and architecture at IIT Roorkee, I realised very early on that I wasn't learning much, given the fact that I came from a family background in real estate and that the practical knowledge I had gained as a kid going around construction sites in hard hats with my father was much more hands-on and helpful than the theoretical knowledge being imparted. Thus, my focus during my undergraduate years at IIT shifted more towards exploring other avenues and overall personality development.

Be it participation in sports (football), voluntary services through the National Service Scheme (NSS) teaching underprivileged students, spending time learning the basics of finance through readings and taking the certification examinations in financial markets conducted by the National Stock Exchange of India, studying for Chartered Financial Analyst (CFA) exams or ideating on some start-up venture of my own.

Essentially, it was a free-flow process of exploring various options available around me, using a hit-and-trial method to find what I could be good at, enjoy and use to create value for myself and the broader ecosystem: the journey to finding my personal ikigai.

After evaluating various courses of action for the journey ahead, I eventually decided to go to HEC Paris School of Management, after landing admission offers from London Business School, HEC Paris and Harvard University. I enrolled in the Masters in Management (Grande École) programme—a two-year management degree with a major in Finance. Studying finance at arguably the best finance programme in the world, in a cohort of students who would likely go on to become CXOs of Fortune 500 companies across the globe, was truly invaluable.

Having tried my hand at various opportunities while shortlisting the next to pursue during the latter part of my time at IIT, I personally felt a pain point and learnt an important lesson: the limited access to entrepreneurial guidance for people looking to start up, not just in India but internationally as well.

Living through the process—from ideation and shortlisting an idea among the many in mind, to conducting detailed desktop research on the chosen idea—the problem, business, market segment, scope and feasibility—and validating it, I realised that one of the major *operational* problems was the lack of guidance at each stage of the entrepreneurial journey. From an idea to validation, to launching a product or service and then scaling the business, guidance was scarce. It was something we did have, to some extent, through the IIT network, but it was not available more broadly to others.

Thus, it made a lot of sense to work on creating such a platform: one that aids the entrepreneurial journey by bringing together all the relevant intel and people across the value chain—entrepreneurs, venture capitalists, talent, subject matter experts—on one platform. A place where an entrepreneur could actually focus on solving real problems instead of getting bogged down in operational inefficiencies or reinventing the wheel.

This was the genesis of BUILD, which I started working on with a few of my B-school friends and classmates at HEC Paris. In simple terms, BUILD was 'Google for Entrepreneurship', a platform where an aspiring entrepreneur could access all possible resources to build a business out of an idea.

BUILD brought together all stakeholders on a unified platform, where one could not just network, review and evaluate different avenues, but also collaborate and work with relevant, interested people across the value chain. It enabled access to the best talent pool, advisors and guidance, while allowing people to share their experiences, so that most of the time was spent on actually solving problems and *building* the business.

Working on this passion project was nothing short of a dream. I juggled coursework in management while spending hours each day building this platform—both physically and online. From ideating and writing on the walls of the entrepreneurship lab at HEC Paris, to eventually setting up a pro-bono entrepreneurship society around it, the learnings were immense. Far more than someone in their mid to late twenties could possibly imagine or derive from a conventional job.

It was a rollercoaster ride of emotions and challenges, but in overcoming them, we were able to create something of value for the ecosystem. At the end of the day, it boils down to operational excellence and the ability to execute rather than *just* ideate.

Underplayed Effect of Luck in Life

The flip side to the story above—and the learning—is equally, if not more, important: the role of luck or destiny. Fortune favours the brave and hardworking, but underplaying the role of luck is humbling, if anything!

Most humble, self-conscious and successful people in the world realise and acknowledge the role of luck—besides their effort and skill—in their success. Be it Jeff Bezos, one of the world's richest men, who happened to ride the internet wave at just the right point in time; or Warren Buffett, who has often acknowledged being born in an era of American prosperity and growth; or more locally, Akshay Kumar, the Indian actor, who openly admits that his break in Bollywood came by chance. He was working as support staff in a production house, coordinating a photoshoot for actor Govinda, when he went to deliver the developed photos and was randomly picked by Govinda for a movie role.

More importantly, Akshay has always accepted that despite many others around him being more handsome or talented, sheer luck played a decisive role in him being noticed.

On the flip side, all of us come across people who everyone agrees had the potential to achieve great things in life and in their fields, but who didn't because they lacked one or more of perseverance, discipline or consistency.

The name of Vinod Kambli comes to mind—an Indian cricketer who grew up and played alongside Sachin Tendulkar, considered the 'God of cricket'. Both came up through the Mumbai junior circuits and debuted for India around the same time. Yet, while Sachin went on to become a living legend, Kambli's career was unremarkable.

And beyond these well-known names, there are also countless others who missed the cut purely because of luck or the lack of it. These people are all around us. Each of us knows someone in our lives as talented as any celebrated success story we've heard of, but who weren't able to gain fame and recognition for whatever reason, and they remain unnamed, uncelebrated.

The Road (not) Taken: Harvard

Very few people in my circles know that I had, out of interest, applied to and got selected at the Harvard Graduate School of Design to pursue a master's degree in architecture and design. The thought process was to go deeper into understanding international real estate and thereafter return to India to work on the family real estate business, growing it further with a broader perspective, vision and plan.

I had accepted the admission offer, submitted the tuition fees and was due to join the incoming class in a few weeks when I was suddenly faced with an unexpected choice: joining the Investment Banking desk at Goldman Sachs. This opportunity came as a complete surprise, given my profile was anything but that of a typical, 'ideal' candidate that a top investment bank would hire.

For context—most investment banks recruit primarily through structured spring insight and summer internship programmes, which lead to their full-time hiring. As for lateral hires, they are usually candidates with prior banking experience at another firm, or those already in finance and only rarely outsiders—barring national services or, in exceptional cases, professional athletes.

Landing the coveted investment banking role at Goldman Sachs London was, for me, one of the pivotal moments in life— where luck played a far greater role than anything else.

Coming from an engineering and architectural education background, with an entrepreneurial stint as my primary work experience, I lacked both a finance education and prior experience in the field. In contrast, I was competing against candidates with bachelor's degrees in finance, economics or related fields— most with a string of internships already under their belt. By all accounts, the odds were stacked firmly against me.

It all began with a study trip to London. As students of the Grande École master's in management programme (majoring in Finance) at HEC Paris, we were visiting investment banks to meet, network and learn from HEC alumni working there.

We happened to be at the Goldman Sachs London offices on the very day of the Alibaba IPO listing. The atmosphere on the trading floor was charged with tense excitement that quickly turned into chaos as markets opened and the stock debuted with gains of over 60 per cent. Whether Goldman had mispriced the IPO or it was just a classic case of euphoric investors chasing Alibaba shares to dizzying highs was debatable. But in that moment, watching everything unfold, I realised, thanks to conversations with people around me, that this truly was one of the most coveted, high-profile jobs in the world.

Researching further about investment banking after this trip, I discovered it was also one of the highest-paying careers globally. Even at the most junior ranks, salaries ranged between $100,000–200,000—packages comparable to those of CXOs in India, without accounting for purchasing power parity. Prestigious firms like Goldman Sachs, Morgan Stanley and JP Morgan formed the crème de la crème of the financial world.

As luck would have it, once back on the HEC Paris campus after that eventful study trip, I decided to apply for investment banking roles at Goldman and a few other bulge-bracket banks. To my complete surprise, I was selected, starting out as an analyst in the Financial Institutions Group (FIG), Europe, Middle East and Africa (EMEA) Investment Banking division at Goldman Sachs.

5

In Gold(Man) We Trust

A Coveted Investment Banking Role[*]

London summers are probably among the best in the world. There's a reason why it's called the 'English summer'—with sub-5–7°C weather during the day, a touch of warm bright sunlight and people basking in the sun in parks, enjoying public spaces, watching cricket, tennis or football, or simply having a beer, grabbing lunch or picnicking with friends, family or colleagues. Despite this rosy backdrop, my time at Goldman was nothing short of outrageous at many levels.

Before starting my job that August, and as clichéd as it may sound, I had just watched *The Wolf of Wall Street*—both versions: the 1980s film starring Charlie Sheen and the more recent one

---

[*] Names of individuals in this chapter have been changed or omitted to protect the identity of the individuals as per confidentiality agreements with Goldman Sachs and Morgan Stanley.

with Leonardo DiCaprio. I had also read investment banking and private equity classics, including *Barbarians at the Gate*, the unofficial bible for anyone inbound to the field.

The precursor to the job was Goldman Sachs' month-long analyst training programme at its headquarters on Wall Street, New York. The official purpose was training and networking with fellow bankers from different divisions of the firm, but as some of us quickly discovered, it turned into largely about partying.

Coming back to start off in London, I experienced first-hand what I had only ever heard of before: the borderline crazy banking hours. We would do 9 a.m. to 3 a.m., averaging sixteen to eighteen hours a day, or ninety to hundred hours a week, including weekends. This was not for days, but for weeks and months—the reality of the initial years for almost all junior bankers. I say 'almost all' because many simply quit or gave up along the way.

We would show up to work at 9 a.m. in sharp suits, spend the day working on business development pitch books, decks (fancy words for basically PowerPoint slides), screen annual reports, company investor presentations, broker research reports and data from the Bloomberg terminal, CapIQ, FactSet and the like.

Thereafter, we would turn around the initial drafts of the deck post internal meetings with MDs and VPs running the business development efforts and live deals through multiple iterations of the deck with comments from all. Building a financial model of the company or a business merger, acquisition, or leveraged buy-out opportunity, attending long all-party calls on deals, meetings with lawyers, accountants and clients whilst working on some or multiple of these—this was our day-to-day life.

For all those of you who found the above few sentences all gibberish, investment banking is essentially a field where people with fancy degrees in finance, accounting, economics and some law, or background in other topical industries, end up working on business advisory. Some less topical outliers are seen as well—liberal arts or history graduates or those from a military background.

The advisory work revolves around helping businesses with growth strategies, acquisitions or mergers with competitors. Meanwhile, other divisions of an investment bank focus on different areas of financial markets: sales and trading (executing trades for institutions, wealth management and other clients or the firm's proprietary investment book), merchant banking, wealth management or private equity groups that invest on behalf of clients and with the bank's own proprietary capital.

Overall, investment banks are structured like vast machines, with people as cogs in the larger scheme. The work feels high-profile—dealing with CXOs of Fortune 500 companies, governments, sovereign wealth funds, billionaires and family offices—but sooner or later, all bankers realise they are replaceable. Everyone is. The system is hierarchical, designed like interlinked cogwheels and even the most 'invincible' people eventually get replaced by someone as qualified and competent, waiting to pounce at the opportunity. It's Darwinism at its peak!

The culture can be borderline toxic, with insecurities running hand in hand with alpha-human egos at every level. Some might argue that the pedantic nature of the work and the grind of rising through the ranks—from analyst to associate, vice president, executive director, managing director and the rare few who make partner—is the only path. And the even rarer few eventually make CXOs.

Goldman Sachs Investment Banking: 'Sexy and I Know It!'

That was the work side of things. On the softer side, the unofficial investment banking starter kit would include Patagonia vests, sharp suits with price tags running into thousands of dollars from Savile Row in London or other bespoke design labels; Gucci, Burberry and Ferragamo belts; Tumi handbags; and $5,000 Rolex, Omega or Rado watches, with more expensive pieces like Patek Philippe for the senior ranks. For women, the range would extend from Louis Vuitton and Hermès Birkin bags to Christian Louboutin heels, Van Cleef accessories and Cartier bracelets.

As an insider, there's an unsaid rule: analysts ideally wouldn't want to wear a watch or accessory from a brand more expensive than what their senior counterparts wear. Essentially, you wouldn't see an analyst flaunting a Patek Philippe when his VP or MD wore a Rolex. Unless, of course, the analyst comes from an influential family with connections—something everyone would already know—in which case (s)he is in the system based on 'rank'. Meritocracy and not-so-meritocracy often coexist even in banking, like everywhere else, as such people (or their families and connections) can bring business for the firm.

So, as an outsider, if you're observant enough, you can usually gauge a banker's level of seniority in public settings simply by noting the thread count or make of their suits, their watch or other accessories. For the curious, there's the *Wall Street Oasis* blog, which is akin to the TV series *Gossip Girl*, but for fashion and insider scoop in investment banking and finance.

Banking has its perks. It comes with expensive annual ski trips to the Swiss or French Alps, where the price for the same set of luxurious amenities is tiered based on seniority. An analyst might pay a minimal amount, while a managing director might pay five to eight times more. Arguably fair, given the skewed compensation structure too! Then there are the £200 steak lunches, dinners for networking or client meetings at the most exclusive restaurants in Mayfair, London, or their equivalents on New York's Upper East Side or Fifth Avenue. Endless parties and after-parties at places like Sushi Samba, Maggie's and other high-end clubs across the city. The £50 daily dinner allowance to order two-to-three-course meals on *Seamless* after 7:30 p.m. at the office, followed by chauffeured rides home in a Mercedes S-Class or BMW 7-Series. Hospitality tickets for 'client entertainment'—English Premier League and Champions League games, Wimbledon, the Chelsea Flower Show—the list goes on.

For those keen to know more, the HBO series *Industry* is worth a watch, essentially glorifying (and almost satirising) the investment banking lifestyle along with its obvious toxicity. For anyone truly considering a career in finance, I would recommend adding to the list *Barbarians at the Gate* (as mentioned earlier), the writings and blog of valuation guru and NYU Stern professor Aswath Damodaran and the TV series *Billions*—loosely inspired by hedge fund mogul Steve Cohen—as part of the starter pack (pun intended).

Overpaid and Overworked: Working with the Best

Despite complaints about the crazy work hours, one could hardly argue against how well the job pays. There are countless instances of people seeing a large sum hit their bank accounts and immediately going on outrageous spending sprees—whether buying Ferraris or Lamborghinis on the day year-end bonus cheques worth hundreds of thousands of pounds were credited, or splurging on uber-luxurious accessories.

The underlying toxicity (the price to pay!) comes with the role. Recall how we used to work 100+ hours a week for months during live deal execution, which is almost always the case for 'good' bankers and rarely so for the 'other' kind once you're internally placed in a category you fall in. If someone doesn't know which category they fall under, chances are they fall into the latter bucket.

Then there's the other side to the long-hours culture: junior bankers 'face-timing'—staying in the office until the early hours of the morning, not necessarily working but projecting an image of being super dedicated and hard working by putting in the 'long-hours'. To preserve their sanity, some even argue (to themselves) that despite being in one of the highest-paying jobs, bankers are still *underpaid* when one normalises for the number of hours they put in at work.

I remember the story of an Indian analyst at Goldman's Silicon Valley office. He came from a humble background, a Marwari from Rajasthan, and despite making a six-figure salary at twenty-two, he struggled to cope with the work hours, the stress and the underlying toxicity. Every time he told his parents back home about his struggles, they urged him to think long term, endure the grind and focus on the career trajectory and financial rewards.

To be fair, anyone joining a new workplace—whether a fresh graduate or a seasoned professional—understands that the initial months (around six, in most firms) are probationary. During this period, errors are usually viewed with empathy; it's the time needed to settle into a new role, adapt to operational demands and become familiar with the organisation. I tell myself that perhaps this analyst's parents assumed the same for their son, that he would overcome this phase. But the reality was that he was bottling everything inside. Unable to cope, he was later found deceased in his apartment building's parking lot, with surveillance confirming his death as a suicide, as per press releases.

My heart sank when I learnt this. The repercussions were enormous. It hit the news everywhere. Inside and outside the finance world, everyone was talking about this young analyst.

Eventually, Goldman mandated Saturdays off for junior bankers, essentially a 'Friday 9 p.m to Sunday 9 a.m. work curfew'. This meant bankers wouldn't work during that thirty-six-hour window unless absolutely necessary, and only with prior approval from the managing director of the relevant business group. The idea was to prevent burnout among junior bankers, to avoid people working like zombies.

No one needs to validate why a weekend is necessary, but such is the workload of junior bankers at investment banks, that the thirty-six-hour work curfew became a *radical* precedent. It was the talk of the town, and eventually, almost all banks adopted some form of protected weekend for junior bankers.

More recently, a few years ago, another incident at Goldman made waves. A junior banker—ironically, the son of a blue-chip private equity firm's CXO—along with colleagues, put together a presentation that showcased the *dark side* of banking: the hundred-hour weeks, the relentless stress, the toxicity of culture and the borderline pedantic activities. Obvious fodder for the press and public debate!

CXOs and other senior bankers came out to defend the culture, saying this is 'how banking has always been' and that everyone in the industry has endured it. It's not a nine-to-five job with work-life balance, they argued, but 'the banking life'. A path only for a very few: those willing to grind hard, endure the downsides and take the ride towards exponential growth in career and financial rewards. The trade-offs are clear—failed marriages, infidelity, insecurities, receding hairlines, social and family sacrifices, declining health.

One particular MD at Goldman Sachs London remains in my memory. Now a partner, and one of the firm's most respected leaders, he would regularly be in his office until 11 p.m. or midnight, dining alone while still working or sometimes watching something on his iPad once the work was done, instead of spending that time back home with his family. Hollow, to say the least.

I am not saying this is true for all senior bankers. Many have better balance, depending on workload. But this MD was an extreme case: someone who dedicated his life to becoming a highly respected banker in the industry, but at an enormous personal cost.

The industry has a strict stance on avoiding office relationships and requires full disclosure to avoid conflicts of interest and/or breach of confidentiality. Despite this, there are some cases of office relationships, across ranks: yup, not just junior bankers or naïve twenty-two-year-olds but even at the highest ranks (obviously hush hush, and it never makes it to press!). This is something which is common in other industries too, but you get the point.

The truth is that many bankers eventually leave after earning enough in a few years to move into private equity, hedge funds or corporate start-ups. Others move into CXO roles in global corporations or government. Well-known examples include Rishi Sunak (former UK Prime Minister), Steven Mnuchin (ex-US Treasury Secretary) and Emmanuel Macron (current President of France and former Rothschild MD). It's the 'revolving doors' dynamic, from banking to government or regulation.

Others simply retire in their forties, worn out from the toll of constant high stress and long hours.

The point I am making here is that the job has its flipside. Many who take this path come from difficult backgrounds or circumstances—those with limited means or from middle-class families—and push harder than most, striving for a better life for themselves and their families. But this comes with a cost: the strain on family, mental health and personal well-being.

As the Bhagavad Gita rightly notes, life's essence lies in balance and equanimity: being able to fulfil one's familial, personal and professional duties; making an impact in the ecosystem; while pursuing the greater purpose of the soul.

If sharing this insider's perspective on banking helps readers or acquaintances better decide whether to tread the investment banking path, or wisely steer away from it, then I would consider my job here done just fine.

Attention to Detail: Primary Facet of Banking Years

Investment banking workstyle is perfectionist, or very 'German', in the sense that everything has to be done in a certain way, to the highest quality standards and strictly as per the hierarchical pecking order.

For instance, for a business development meeting deck, the MD would share his thoughts, the VP would build a strawman or a storyline shell around it and then the associate and analyst would add the heart, meat and bones using data, analyses and numbers to bring the deck to life.

Essentially, the analyst would work on the deck and/or financial model based on comments from the MD and VP; the associate would check the analyst's work; and the VP would be the one presenting and leading the client-facing interactions and running the deal.

Attention to detail is therefore one of the primary facets of being a banker—if not the most important one—across all workstreams, since the toolkit (presentation decks, financial models, number crunching and everything hands-on) is under the analyst's control.

It could mean working throughout the day on turning the VP's comments on a deck, and then late night on the MD's comments—aka that dreaded 'pls fix' email. Or ensuring that everything is consistent across the deck. Even the font size of the footnotes! Not seven or five—but specifically size six. No double spaces between words. No typos. And certainly no 'schoolboy errors' such as colour-coding mix-ups in Excel backup files—where hardcoded numbers are shown in dark blue, formulas in black, complex cell references or external references in red—or mistakes like not saving files in the correct filename format, not versioning up or accidentally replying to all instead of a specific recipient in emails.

Even the deal toys (mementos, similar to awards or trophies showcasing the completion of a deal—usually designed in some form linked to the underlying business, complete with bank and advisor logos) are subject to scrutiny. The font sizes and the order of names in the working group lists (records of all people involved in a deal, across clients, banks, law firms, tax and advisory firms) matter greatly. It's all fundamentally *attention-to-detail* driven.

Despite seeming borderline pedantic, the very nature of investment banking work makes one more aware, more mindful and appreciative of accuracy. It sharpens the habit of noticing details in everything, something that pays off in the long term. As the saying goes: *the devil is in the detail.*

Personally, one of my most embarrassing moments as an analyst, which taught me attention to detail the hard way and a lesson that stayed with me, occurred in my early days. Goldman was working with the United Kingdom's Her Majesty's Revenue and Customs Department (UK HMRC), essentially the UK government's finance department, advising them regarding their stake sale (shareholding) in Lloyd's of London and the Royal Bank of Scotland (RBS).

One day, while writing an email to the CEO of RBS, I mistakenly ended my signature with a typo: 'Kid regards' instead of 'Kind regards'. And I hadn't run spellcheck. Wow, my heart sank 30 seconds after sending it, when I re-read the email in my 'sent' folder, but by then, it was too late to recall that email. To make things worse, all the senior Goldman bankers—partners, MDs, VPs—were cc'ed on the email. Within minutes, I received a reply from RBS' CEO: 'Thanks, Kid!' I sank deep into my chair.

I may have glorified the incident and laugh about it now, but the learning has stayed with me forever.

Right Attitude, Learning Mindset, Hard Work and Dedication

I would eventually go on to work on some of the best investment banking deals across Europe, and some of the largest globally (in terms of deal size), during this time, for instance: initial public offerings (IPOs) and mergers & acquisitions advisory to UK and Irish banking and financial services players such as Shawbrook Bank UK, Richard Branson's Virgin Money Bank, Metro Bank UK, insurance giants such as Zurich Insurance Group, Aviva Plc and the largest stock exchanges of the world, such as Deutsche Börse and the London Stock Exchange. Other deals included working with the UK government through their UK Financial Investments entity (UKFI) for their stake in Lloyd's Bank and Royal Bank of Scotland, as well as with Irish banks such as Bank of Ireland and Allied Irish Banks, among others.

Whether it is sheer luck or a coherent mix of hard work, dedication, discipline and consistency catalysed by luck, it is better expressed through consistent success: are you a one-trick pony or a consistent winner?

But I can certainly vouch that the people and the team I worked with played a big role in shaping my experiences. The journey had its moments: from working on the $21 billion merger of equals between the London Stock Exchange (LSE) and Deutsche Börse (the largest investment banking deal globally at that time!), which was eventually called off by regulators for competitive reasons (concerns of cannibalisation from Europe's two largest exchanges merging), to working on the IPO of UK and Europe's first dog-friendly bank, Metro Bank UK. The bank's chairman and founder, Vernon Hill, adored his dog, treating him like his own child. It was no surprise then that, during pre-IPO roadshow meetings, he once called off a full day of investor meetings because his dog wasn't feeling well. The timing was not ideal, especially as some colleagues had flown from London to New York only to find roadshow meetings cancelled. Not the best ego massage that an MD at Goldman would want, especially after knowing the reason behind the cancellation!

Another memory is the secondary equity placement of Shawbrook Bank, whose CEO, Steve Pateman, was also a friend of my professor and thesis guide at HEC Paris. When I arrived at Shawbrook's office, Steve recognised me and joked with our MD that he had brought along a 'friendly face'. Such is the power of the HEC network!

There were other deals too, in the collateralised debt obligations (CDOs) and collateralised loan obligations (CLOs) segment—the infamous monsters of the 2008 global financial crisis, which some may recall thanks to *The Wolf of Wall Street*.

All these deals happened in less than eighteen months, and looking back, I realise how this shaped a name on the street: you earn credibility when you punch above your weight and put in the effort without holding back. Thus came the evolution of our so-called 'dream team': Jake Byrne, then MD and COO at Goldman's Financial Institutions Group (FIG) EMEA Investment Banking; Ryan Boyle, then VP, now MD at Goldman Sachs FIG EMEA; Jonathan English, then associate at Goldman

Sachs FIG EMEA, today Portfolio Manager at Steve Cohen's celebrated investment office, Point72; and yours truly.

For those unfamiliar, Steve Cohen is the billionaire hedge fund manager who famously made a fortune during the 2008 financial crisis. He is such a legend that HBO's long-running series *Billions* is loosely inspired by his life.

Here, I also draw a parallel with Indian cricketer Yuvraj Singh, one of the game's finest all-rounders. During the 2011 Cricket World Cup, Yuvraj carried India through to the finishing line in crucial matches, excelling in both batting and bowling and eventually won the *Man of the Series* award, having helped India lift the World Cup after a gap of twenty-eight years. It was later revealed that he had been so sick at the time that he would sometimes vomit the night before matches, yet performed under the sheer pressure of 1.4 billion expectations! I didn't fully appreciate the gravity of this situation until I experienced something faintly similar. Not that grand per se, but enough for me to empathise and appreciate what he might have been going through.

During the LSE–Deutsche Börse merger deal, I would sometimes find myself throwing up at 3 or 4 a.m. in the office, overwhelmed at the thought that, as an analyst, I was working directly with a VP (Ryan), and we were running this $21 billion deal, the largest in investment banking till that date!

It's rare in life to find people who value you, your contributions, who are keen on working with you and most importantly, with whom *you* get along. It feels like winning a lottery, or plain luck, to end up in such a setup. The counter-view, however, is that it isn't luck—it's about having the right attitude and mindset, which lands you such opportunities in the first place.

I fondly remember the days when my VP, Ryan, would sit with me at 3 a.m. and work on my system, teaching me how to build a financial model for a bank. The balance sheet of banks is completely the opposite to that of a typical firm—for instance, loans are *assets* for banks but *liabilities* for businesses. I often wondered why a VP, who could easily have gone home at 9 or 10 p.m. after a twelve-hour day—was choosing to sit at my desk and teach me. Eventually, Ryan told me it was my 'right attitude' that pushed him to invest his time. To paraphrase him: there are many smart people in banking, coming from the best business schools, but very few come with the right attitude, a learning mindset, who don't shy away from and are dedicated to work.

Attention to detail is what I learnt from Ryan—how he would literally spend an hour or so reviewing my work, writing back an email with his comments and telling me to fix the font size of the footnote from size 7 to 6 or where there was double spacing in the text of a slide in my presentation deck or to fix the colour of some key message in a slide to GS style (*Gstyle format* in Goldman language).

It was 2–3 a.m. on a workday when I received another one of these emails from Ryan about a pitch deck we were working on. Seeing him walk past me, probably heading home, while I was reading his email, I walked him to the office elevators and towards the taxi waiting outside Goldman's office on Fleet Street.

On the way out, I asked him why he spent an hour writing word-for-word corrections—finding minor mistakes (to my mind) in my work and then sending me an email to correct them rather than fixing them himself in probably ten minutes. His response, funnily enough, was, 'Because I'm a VP and you're the analyst. More importantly, it's to teach you attention to detail—to check, recheck and check again for consistency before sending it to your senior. It's about valuing the quality of both your work and your senior's time.'

Wow. It was like a friendly slap in the face. He didn't intend it harshly, but it woke me up, literally and figuratively, and the lesson has stayed with me forever.

Later at Morgan Stanley, and even today at Bimtek, I still fondly tell this story to younger colleagues as a guidepost, and each time I do, it brings a smile to my face. I try to do the same that Ryan did for me: invest in the right people.

One key learning for any junior person: your job is to make your senior's life easier. This is the unsaid KRA of excelling at work. Not politics. Not showmanship. Just this. Especially in a meritocratic set-up like Goldman and investment banking, but equally true in any field.

No surprise, then, that Ryan and I developed a mentor–mentee relationship—a bond somewhat like Harvey and Mike from *Suits*. Ryan was not only a rockstar professionally but also someone admirable in personal life. From excelling at work, grooming the simpletons such as myself, spending time with his daughter and his wife, to walking his dogs, picking up laundry and tending to family obligations—he was, and remains, the role model one could hope for.

Despite 90–100-hour weeks and handling multiple live deals at once, I could have taken the relatively easier but still not easy route that most analysts would take, namely, getting in the sleep hours whenever there was downtime or sleeping more than four hours on a usual day. But Ryan reinforced in me that beyond execution, one must cultivate the learning mindset, independent thinking and clarity of thought. He urged me to make time to read widely on my own, contextualise the deals we were working on, essentially being on top of the work and its significance in the bigger scheme of things and to understand sectors, segments, industries and trends—to not just do (or simply be the 'hands' at work), but also *think*.

Looking back now, I can see the difference: an analyst who only 'does' models and decks versus an analyst who adds value by understanding *why* and *what for*. Going through the grind, working and keeping my eyes and ears open so as to not just 'do' but also think and learn made all the difference. Ryan was grooming me to be a version of himself. In hindsight, he helped me reconnect with the very lessons I learnt at Vidyamandir: consistency, depth of understanding, a learning mindset and independent thinking.

Overall, the key takeaways remain: attention to detail, the right work attitude and clear communication. These three skills, on top of technical proficiency (corporate finance concepts, economics, Excel modelling, PowerPoint, Microsoft Office execution), are what make someone excel in the world of finance.

To be fair, these skills are transferable to *any* career or industry. They are universal foundations that set you on the right path—upwards and onwards!

Too Good to Be True, Yet True? Definitely God's Grace!

An analyst usually spends about three-and-a-half years before being promoted to associate. The same applies to an associate, who spends about three-and-a-half or four years before making VP and then another three years before becoming executive director, followed by another three or four years before finally reaching MD (or longer—and, in some cases, being shown the door if one isn't likely to make it). Thereafter, with time, one could be considered for partner at the bank.

Such is the power of compounding and focusing on simple, basic building blocks that I ended up being promoted to associate in just eighteen months (a full two years ahead of time!)—and later, from associate to VP in similar fashion.

It's experiences like these that humble you, making you realise that God indeed has a plan for all of us. Eventually, hard work, consistency and dedication do catch up. The number of deals I worked on, and the experiences I had at Goldman, would typically take someone more than four or five years, and they would have to go through the grind and rise through the ranks for them. Blessed and grateful are the right words to describe this phase of my career.

> **Life Lesson #10:** Practise consistency, discipline and patience, both in personal and professional life.

We've spoken about this earlier in the book, but the seed for this lesson was planted during my time working with and learning under Ryan. By seeing him conduct himself as the best version of himself: a rockstar at work, and equally a great husband, father, son and family man outside of it.

> **Life Lesson #11:** The right attitude and mindset eventually catch up with you and your career path, no matter what and where you start from.
>
> **Life Lesson #12:** Put your head down in the early years, go through the grind and don't run after money—it eventually catches up in the medium term.

Keeping our heads down and being faithful to our deeds is central, or as the Bhagavad Gita notes, 'Work is worship'.

I am a firm believer in the idea that no matter what happens, our dedication and quality of work should never be compromised, whether due to issues at work, difficult people or situations or even external life factors.

An MD at Goldman Sachs London, once casually told me over coffee: 'No matter what is going on in any part of your life, do not let your work suffer.' I was in awe of his dedication and focus. No wonder he rose through the ranks in such a competitive environment, from starting as an associate to recently becoming partner at the firm.

It's these right building blocks that, when focused upon, lead to quality of work, steep learning curves and, eventually, rising through the ranks—and of course, the outsized financial rewards that follow.

This truth applies to *any* field, because it's during the initial years of struggle, learning and grind that one builds the foundation. In the medium term, career trajectory and monetary success take care of themselves.

6

Meeting the Anchor and Soulmate

Wherever I am and whatever I am doing in life, credit goes more to my partner than to me, to be fair. She is the anchor of my life. I am an old-school person who believes that coming back home to someone you can trust like the back of your hand is a blessing. To my mind, the peace and sanctity at home are as important as hard work and dedication at work in driving one's success. It is with this calm and balance at home that one can centre oneself, achieve equanimity and then go out to fight the supposed battles at work and focus on all the other aspirations in life.

To see someone smile—and to know that you are the reason for that smile—is pure bliss. This book is neither a romantic comedy nor a love story, but it is, in all honesty, a man acknowledging the efforts and influence of someone in his life.

As a kid, I watched the Tom Cruise-starrer *The Last Samurai*. It didn't strike me then, but when I watched it again later in life, I realised one key learning. While training Captain Nathan

Algren (Tom Cruise), the Samurai master advises him to 'fight with no mind'. Not in the literal sense, but metaphorically—he was guiding Algren to stop being distracted by everything else, and with a clear head, focus entirely on the battle at hand. Against the backdrop of scenes in the film—where men are falling, cut into pieces like cucumbers and carrots in a salad—we see how, with this precision and clarity of thought, Tom Cruise's character is able to anticipate the moves and attacks of the opponent and visualise the imminent series of battle events in his head even before the fight begins.

It's like battles are won outside the battlefield—within the mind.

A Better Man—The Half That Makes Me Full, Each Day

Sometimes, whilst pursuing excellence, it can easily happen that we become ruthless and stop thinking about our people or the human side of things. I had fallen into this bucket earlier. No shame in putting my hand up, acknowledging it and course-correcting. This is why I feel that those who end up with partners who make them better at everything in life, just by their presence, are truly lucky.

During my days at Goldman, I would get so absorbed in work that I started missing family events, including birthdays. And for those who think that's fine, I don't mean missing the celebrations, but the bare minimum of even *wishing* family on their birthdays! Working sixteen to eighteen hours a day without time to eat properly, or eating at my desk while working, is one thing. But missing loved ones' birthdays altogether is another.

I remember once, it was my sister's birthday and I completely forgot to call or text her. She called me a couple of times, which I missed. On the fourth attempt, my assistant, Hannah, picked up and transferred the call to me, saying 'Family'. Hannah came in to make sure I answered and heard my sister tell me these exact words: 'Hey Mohit. Sorry, I know you're very busy, so I thought I'd call and quickly wish myself. A very happy birthday to me!'

Ouch. What a slap in the face! Though I immediately asked Hannah to pick up a gift for her and handed over my credit card, the judgement on Hannah's face—and the figurative slap ringing in my ears from my sister's words—took a long time to sink in.

But that's what some successful, albeit work-obsessed, people tend to be like. Recently, I met the CXO of one of the world's largest real estate private equity firms. He told me that during a visit to their India offices, he advised junior and mid-level bankers to absorb their work so deeply in their subconscious minds that they might as well even dream about it! His view was that this is how one begins to see every possible risk factor in deals and plan to mitigate them.

I had passively learnt that this was the case for some of the world's most celebrated figures such as Warren Buffett, Elon Musk, Jeff Bezos.

Take Buffett. While undeniably brilliant and gifted, his biography also documents how his marriage with Suzie fell apart. Suzie had essentially become just one piece of the puzzle in his life—a backbone supporting him emotionally, raising their kids, handling all the family duties—until, eventually, they drifted apart and she began dating her workout coach. One of the most successful investors on earth ended up with a failed marriage—it makes one wonder about the humaneness behind an anchor or a successful marriage.

Elon Musk, widely admired as the richest man in the world, has an equally turbulent personal story. From PayPal to Tesla and SpaceX, his journey from near-bankruptcy to becoming a billionaire is iconic. Along the way, however, he divorced, remarried and entered multiple relationships, ultimately fathering children with different partners but never having a stable marriage.

Jeff Bezos, founder of Amazon, had something similar. His split with Mackenzie Scott, in what became a $38 billion divorce settlement, was headline news. Later, he even commented that the woman he was with made him feel alive and young again, and so he was happy.

Back home in India, Sachin Tendulkar, a cricket legend, was depicted in his biopic through his wife's words: that he was 'too big' for his familial duties. She casually remarked that she never expected him to help with basic parenting tasks or household chores—feeding the children, changing diapers or anything most of us would consider normal. His duty, instead, was to bear the weight of over a billion Indians' hopes on his shoulders.

I am not criticising. These are national and international heroes, titans in their fields. My point is simpler: sometimes it is the *little things* that bring true meaning to life. That's what we lose sight of when too absorbed in work or a particular pursuit. Stepping away at times, engaging in a different, refreshing endeavour, can reset our perspectives and help us return with clarity.

For instance, take a counter-example: Mahendra Singh Dhoni, another cricketing legend and one of India's most successful captains. In his biopic, during a lean patch in form, Dhoni is shown returning to his other passion—cars and bikes. He would spend hours tinkering in his garage, fixing mechanical issues, greasing parts, while subconsciously drawing parallels to his cricket technique and realising flaws he hadn't noticed earlier while playing.

That break rejuvenated him. He corrected his game and went on to lead India to victory in the 2011 World Cup, cementing his reputation as one of the greatest captains across all formats—aptly nicknamed 'Captain Cool' for his unshakable calm demeanour.

Marriage: The Single Biggest Decision in Life

Charlie Munger once famously said that marriage is one of the most important decisions a person makes in their life. Warren Buffett, in his own blunt way, said that if your marriage is built around a piece of paper filled with detailed terms and conditions (a pre-nuptial agreement), then you might as well not do it at all.

I couldn't agree more with these legends. It really is as simple as being with someone you truly connect with—mentally, emotionally, spiritually and in terms of values. The person you share your life with, and build your family with, matters more than anything else in shaping the long-term trajectory of your life, your experiences, your path and your achievements.

> **Life Lesson #13:** It's the big decisions in life that matter in the long run.

Marriage is one of them. Others include the family we are born into, the schools we attend, the career paths we pursue—these are among the most fundamental decisions that shape the course of our lives. It's like the Pareto Principle at play: 80 per cent of our results and outcomes are driven by 20 per cent of our decisions and actions.

> **Life Lesson #14:** *'Jeevan madhya me hai'* or, as the saying goes, life's essence lies in balance. It's important to maintain equanimity and avoid extremes that stretch a person beyond their means.

7

Morgan Stanley

Dumb Luck or a Blend of Consistency, Discipline and Patience with Some Luck?[*]

HAVING WORKED IN INVESTMENT BANKING FOR A COUPLE OF years and been fortunate enough to probably work with and learn from some of the best in the industry and having worked on some of the largest deals in banking and financial services across Europe, I had had this steep learning curve over a short time-span, which seemed too good to be true.

Against the backdrop of my successful stint at Goldman, I realised that perhaps the best time to step away from FIG investment banking would be now (then)—at a career high at

---

[*] Names of individuals in this chapter have been changed or omitted to protect the identity of the individuals as per confidentiality agreements with Goldman Sachs and Morgan Stanley.

Goldman—and pursue something aligned with my long-term interests, rather than risk sliding into complacency.

Thus, it made sense to transition to my always-preferred sector: real estate and broader infrastructure. This move, from Goldman Sachs to Morgan Stanley Real Estate, was in essence a step in the right direction towards my eventual transition and move back to India, where I envisioned working on my own investment office across real estate and capital markets.

Goldman Sachs and Morgan Stanley—both being among the top three names in the business and often mentioned in the same breath—operate with starkly contrasting cultures.

At Goldman Sachs, we were often referred to on the street as 'Goldman Pricks'—people considered the best in the business but carrying a cocky 'sexy and I know it' attitude and air about themselves. The culture was about being the best at everything, at almost any cost—not unethical per se, but pushing boundaries to every possible extent to stay at the top.

By contrast, Morgan Stanley was known for being about *doing the right thing*—for stakeholders, clients, employees, colleagues and, by extension, for the firm itself.

Of course, there was much in common as well. Both had the same internal politics at peer and hierarchical levels, with the same insecurities bred by the ultra-competitive environment and the clash of alpha egos.

At Morgan Stanley, I primarily focused on UK and EMEA real estate, working with sovereign wealth funds such as the Canadian Pension Plan Investment Board (CPPIB) for their real estate and infrastructure investments across Europe. I also worked on certain segments of real estate with clients such as Unibail-Rodamco-Westfield (the world's largest shopping mall operator), the Fawaz Al-Hokair Group (Saudi royalty-owned

Arabian Centres Company and the Middle East's largest commercial real estate player), among others.

Sovereign wealth funds are investment organisations set up by countries to manage state capital by investing across asset classes and geographies. This is done both through direct investments and indirectly through capital allocations to celebrated global investment houses such as Blackstone and Brookfield, as well as to not-so-celebrated but upcoming fund managers and investment houses such as Bimtek (of yours truly). For context, most developed nations operate under a net cash surplus scenario. Their annual revenue from taxes and other state endeavours exceeds the government's annual expenses—including those for growth, development and defence. A share of this surplus is reinvested in GDP-boosting growth initiatives, while another share is allocated to global investments.

Similarly, many top university endowment funds operate under a surplus. After covering operating expenses and scholarships, surplus income is invested via their endowment funds, both directly and indirectly, on a similar basis as sovereign wealth funds.

Some of the other institutional investors include insurance companies that deploy the surplus generated from premiums collected, adjusted for (minus) the claims settled; and workforce pension or welfare funds, such as the Ontario Teachers' Pension Plan Board. Together, sovereign wealth funds, university endowments, insurance companies, family offices of billionaires and ultra-HNIs and similar entities constitute the institutional investor base.

Delving Deeper into Ideas and Execution

My time at Morgan Stanley was more focused on applying the learnings from Goldman to run end-to-end investment live deal executions, build investor relationships, as well as focus on team building, junior banker training and business development.

Headcount churn at the junior level is an industry norm in banking and finance, making it critical to hire, train and retain the best junior bankers as an investment in the overall ecosystem. People leave banking for various reasons: switching from smaller boutiques (such as Lazard or Evercore) to Top-3 bulge bracket banks (Goldman, Morgan Stanley, JP Morgan); moving from a Top-3 to private equity funds, hedge funds or technology start-ups; or even starting their own ventures.

Exit opportunities are plenty if you are a good banker. Otherwise, average bankers get stuck, rising slowly through the ranks after grinding it out or being shown the door, politely nudged out with negligible or zero bonuses (the firm's way of asking you to leave 'gracefully'). Rising from a junior to a senior banker role is a shift from execution-driven, hands-on work to more 'brains' or strategy-driven work—business development, deal execution, process management and the sales side of the business.

Grooming junior bankers thus became an additional responsibility I was asked to handle at Morgan Stanley—conducting interviews, visiting university and business school campuses for career fairs, hiring and networking events and hand-holding interns, analysts and associates through business development, deal flows and execution training.

On the execution side, understanding the mindset and investment 'underwrite' of various investor bases and the bells and whistles to each specific investor is an art that I did pick up on. 'Underwrite' is a financial term that indicates a scenario wherein an investor puts together their investment thesis, strategy and the underlying assumptions driving the said investment.

On the execution side, I came to understand the mindset and investment underwrite of various investor bases, and the bells and whistles particular to each as a fine art.

As simple as it sounds, enormous energy (read: calories) is burnt in boardrooms and outside leveraging expertise across ranks and industry, engaging consultants, advisors, lawyers and bankers to ensure an investment case is air-tight, backed by precision and aligned with investor, fund and limited partner (LP) base to generate sensible risk-adjusted returns. This isn't meant as a primer on underwriting, but to illustrate how multi-billion-dollar deals are driven by six-decimal-point-level granularity, precision in numbers on Excel and the clarity of thought, a diligent investment process and across risk scenarios behind them.

One such mandate was the UK's third-largest purpose-built student accommodation platform, Liberty Living (LL), backed by CPPIB (Canadian Pension Plan Investment Board) monies. Purpose-built student accommodation is an asset class where students live in dorm-style facilities with world-class infrastructure, either on or around campus in the university catchment areas. These were developed, some acquired and all operated and managed under a platform model. LL reached a ~$5 billion enterprise value with ~25,000 beds across major UK education hubs. We eventually exited by selling it to Unite Group, the UK's largest student accommodation platform, which expanded from ~50,000 to ~75,000 beds post-acquisition.

Side note: cultural toxicity, egos and politics had their place just fine at Morgan Stanley, too. While working on an investment deal for a Canadian institutional investor alongside Middle Eastern sovereign wealth funds, egos clashed across ranks amongst the three bulge brackets involved: Goldman

Sachs, Morgan Stanley and JP Morgan. This is a classic tussle across investment banks wherein the best interests of a client are kept at heart and the best inputs, advisory outputs from each and reputations at stake. *Supposed mediocrity* can sometimes drive *supposed smart people* insane. Banking is filled with hyper-smart people boasting degrees from the best institutions. Yet, when they come together, borderline 'dumb' acts of some can drive others insane. For example, I recall a boardroom session with an FTSE 100 company, discussing their long-range business plan and growth strategy. Out of nowhere, an MD from a top bank (which was in the news at the time for acquiring a troubled Swiss bank) made such a bizarre, random comment that my MD and I gasped. Controlling the laughter, I stepped out into another room to laugh it off, only to be joined seconds later by my MD, who pretended to excuse himself to the washroom but joined me instead and burst out laughing.

When we returned to the meeting, we realised the walls were not soundproof. The looks on everyone's faces told us that they had likely pieced it all together! The poor MD's face went crimson-pink when he caught on. Needless to say, I avoided making eye contact with him for the rest of the meeting.

Then there was a French executive director at Morgan Stanley: highly skilled, technically brilliant, but infamous for his temper. Odd as it sounds, he and I became close friends. One evening, while working late, he asked me to accompany him for a smoke. The boring person that I am, I do not smoke or consume alcohol or any other substance. Him asking me despite knowing that I don't smoke reminded me of the MBA school's 'signalling theory' soft signs, so there I was with him, walking out.

We went to the roof of the Morgan Stanley building at Canary Wharf. To my shock, he casually walked right to the edge and screamed his lungs out. It would not be an exaggeration to say that I imagined my world collapsing in those few seconds—him jumping and me being framed as the one who pushed him! The headlines, my family's shame, my ruined life—it all played out in my mind before he casually turned around, calm as ever, and started chatting about life and work as if nothing had happened. When I confronted him, he shrugged it off, saying he was irritated by some colleagues' 'stupidity' and needed to vent it out. I genuinely didn't know whether to laugh, curse him or punch him for nearly giving me a heart attack. In the end, we just laughed it off and have been the thickest of friends.

To be fair, I, too, have had my moments of irritation when sometimes some of the smartest around pull up something that just makes you gape. Once, while working on a live deal with other banks (bankers) over at our offices, we were discussing the financial knitty-gritty and I did a quick mental math calculation ($15 \times 21 = 315$) aloud and continued the discussion—only to be interrupted by a senior banker from another bank. He rummaged nervously through his bag, pulled out his phone, opened his calculator, typed in the numbers, and, staring wide-eyed, announced, 'Wow, you must be a genius!'

I wasn't sure whether to take it as sarcasm or that basic fifth-grade maths appeared like rocket science to someone earning a seven-figure salary. So yes—to be fair to the French executive director—I could almost empathise.

That said, we became 'partners in crime' too, in borderline food theft! Banks have a food allowance and cab reimbursement policy after 7:30 p.m. in the office. But often, even eating at your desk is rare during marathon working hours, leave aside stepping away for food.

One evening, we ordered food from Shake Shack. Engrossed in work while cold-towelling a financial model for a deal, we lost track of time and got up from our desks at 2 a.m.! Almost five hours after we ordered, we went down to the lobby to pick it up, only to find two other deliveries from Shake Shack sitting there. Hungry and exhausted, we finished our burgers and then gobbled the other two meals as well, assuming they were unclaimed. The next morning, we discovered they belonged to two of our own analysts working late. That sinking feeling when you realise that under the influence of Maslow's pyramid of needs, we ended up eating our colleague's food and not what we assumed it to be (belonging to someone who missed picking up their food earlier and might have gone home already), was a low moment. A few days later, taking them both out for a £200 steak dinner helped partially drown the guilt, but only partially. The rest of it lives on rent-free in my heart till date.

One of the major takeaways of Morgan Stanley, however, was exposure to the ultra-wealthy—the billionaires, their lives, mindsets and thought processes and some key business and operational insights.

For instance, I recall spending time with the son-in-law of the promoter of one of India's largest telecom operator, a multi-billion-dollar enterprise. He built a hotel chain, Hoxton Hotels, which owned the hotel properties and managed them through Ennismore, his hospitality management firm which operated properties such as Hoxton and Gleneagles (another of his hotel brands) across prime European markets. Despite having a billion-dollar capital line through his father-in-law's family office and credit lines against these existing assets, he still sought the kick of having a top private equity fund like Blackstone or Brookfield as an investor to bankroll the US growth plans.

This brought to mind Warren Buffett's famous teaching: why capital allocation is the single biggest responsibility of an investor, owner, operator or business promoter. Sometimes, however, egos, empire-building desire and the lure of shiny-articles and media coverage overshadow rational decision-making, often leading to *capital erosion* or less-than-ideal business endeavours.

Arabian Nights (and Days)

On the other end of my experiences with the uber-rich were the Middle Eastern royalty and princes, with their oil-driven fortune, empires and lifestyles that could blow anyone's mind. Their desire to own crown-jewel assets across the world, or to build the most luxurious and iconic properties and experiences in the Middle East to showcase to the world, was often just the starting point.

While working on the IPO of Arabian Centres Company (ACC), part of the Fawaz Al-Hokair Group of Saudi Arabia, I witnessed something I could not have imagined in my wildest dreams. It's one thing to run a deal and build an 'equity story' around a business—potential growth scenarios, preparing blue-sky short- and medium-term plans to arrive at a fair valuation range of the business and, thus, price and underwrite the IPO. And thereafter marketing the company through management meetings and global roadshows to test investor appetite before finally listing it on the stock exchange. It's a completely different thing, however, when it becomes a chicken-and-egg problem: reverse-engineering valuation around the number the owners want—predetermined regardless of bankers' advice (which, ironically, is what we are paid for!).

Our EMEA head of real estate and a few colleagues were flying from London to Riyadh to meet the royalty: sheikh, and the ACC management team. Only after boarding the plane did we realise that Mohammed bin Salman (MBS), Crown Prince of Saudi Arabia, had just detained several leading sheikhs and put them under 'private observation' at the Four Seasons Hotel in Riyadh.

This happened to be the very hotel we were booked in during our visit. We sat through the flight nervously, contemplating worst-case scenarios, both for the business and for ourselves. Upon landing in Riyadh, we promptly took the next flight back to London. This was, quite frankly, the safest and sanest thing to do!

Naturally, the deal went quiet for a few quarters after that. When it eventually resumed, we learnt that the IPO was back on because the proceeds were needed to pay the relevant 'ransom' to MBS. The business was now seeking to dilute a fixed equity stake in order to raise the required funds.

It took nearly a year of working with the business and management to reach the business scale and align the medium-term business plan—including the secured assets pipeline, medium-term growth and a directional long-term plan—with the valuation ask of the owners. Only then could we structure and safely underwrite the IPO at the price sought, and market this to leading institutional investors globally.

At the time, the Middle East still followed a Sunday–Thursday work week. For months, I would fly to Dubai or Riyadh on Saturdays, work there until Thursday, then fly back to London in time to spend Fridays in the office. Finally, on Friday night, I would get to sleep in my bed at my London apartment. I would then spend Saturday reading deal documents on my iPad with a coffee in Regent's Park, feeding ducks and taking a walk, before boarding another Saturday night flight back to the Middle East for the Sunday start of the week there.

This went on for months at a stretch. As glamorous as it sounds—five-star hotels and business-class flights—such constant travel can crush the soul of even the most seasoned banker when done back-to-back for an extended period. It's no surprise that bankers and consultants collect passport stamps, hotel points and air miles … but rarely get time to redeem them.

Despite Dubai and Riyadh boasting skylines that spark envy around the world, at times they would make me feel borderline depressed. Picture this: I was staying in an eighty-third-floor suite at the Four Seasons, looking out at sprawling skyscrapers interspersed across endless 'brown'. *Brown* is the colloquial (less-than-polite) way of referring to the landscape—all sand, with buildings painted brown unless they were glass-façade towers. Sand, after all, is not scarce there! The view from up there could challenge anyone's sanity if they weren't acclimatised with the Middle Eastern landscape.

Despite the uber luxurious amenities, infrastructure and externalities, Saudi Arabia has elements which could be culturally jarring. Restaurants and public areas were divided into male-only and family sections; a single man or groups of men were restricted from entering the family sections. Arabian Centres, in fact, made history as the first in the Kingdom to bring *Cineplex* and thus the multiplex experience to Saudi Arabia, besides introducing Western luxury brands such as Louis Vuitton, Burberry, Gucci and Prada through its malls.

Women had only recently been granted permission to drive. Homes were typically built with minimal or no windows, sometimes resembling Soviet-era blocks (with snipers on top; pun intended), adding a sense of bleakness in contrast to the glitzy towers. Alcohol remains strictly banned, as does adultery, although just across the border in Lebanon, such activities are readily available, making it a common weekend getaway for leisurely activities.

And yet, within the walls of the ultra-wealthy, it was an entirely different reality. Rules seemed not to apply—private parties with free-flowing alcohol; gold-plated phones, watches and even cars; wild animals like tigers and lions kept as pets; and, of course, adultery behind closed doors. The Netflix show *Dubai Bling* scratches the surface of this world, but the true excesses of the royalty and uber-rich—their gatherings, events and grandeur or excesses—are so surreal that they force you to stop and reflect.

Learning Softer Aspects of Work

Most business deals are struck over brunches, lunches, dinners and drinks at some of the fanciest places during these networking sessions.

I have been part of many such occasions: spending time in the Morgan Stanley townhouse with the firm's partners, networking with CXOs of the world's most influential firms at the Chelsea Flower Show, playing a round of golf at a private course, attending a Champions League football night or sitting in box seats at Wimbledon. The softer aspects of business conduct remain consistent across geographies; the events and locations may change, but the intent remains the same.

Overall, my time at Morgan Stanley was spent deepening my understanding of the European real estate market, grasping various investor thought processes and sharpening my mindset towards investment management.

As the saying goes, 'Real estate is super local'. This essentially means that while one may understand the theoretical aspects of real estate, markets are inherently local and on-the-ground understanding of each market is critical. Another timeless principle is that location is key in real estate. An on-ground understanding of these two aspects—locality and location— forms the pillar of understanding real estate across geographies.

> **Life Lesson #15:** Every field of work or domain can be simplified into a few building blocks that define one's grasp and, thus, one's success in it.

It is common that when starting to learn about a sector or field, we encounter what feels like hundreds of moving parts and concepts defining it. But deeper analysis reveals that a handful of (likely three or four) pivotal factors usually drive the directional sense with a great degree of accuracy. Almost all the other hundreds of factors are essentially derivatives, expressed in various permutations and combinations of these core drivers.

Albert Einstein once said that one should simplify a process or problem to the point that even a six-year-old can understand it. Simplify any further, and you risk losing the essence.

Virender Sehwag, one of the most explosive batsmen the game of cricket has ever seen, often compared to the legendary Sir Vivian Richards of the West Indies, once explained how he approached batting in the simplest possible way. When facing a delivery, he put it into one of three categories: a ball to be hit, a ball to be defended or a ball to be left. As simple as that. This clarity transformed his career. While others would crumble under pressure, you would see Sehwag playing his strokes as if he were enjoying a casual game with friends in the park, not competing in a high-stakes international match.

It is this clarity and simplicity of thought process that has a magical effect, enabling consistency, impact and repeatable performance across any field of work.

My time at Morgan Stanley further reinforced the belief that while luck plays a pivotal (and often underappreciated) role in where we end up in life, success is more fundamentally linked to keeping our heads down and working consistently, with discipline and patience. This is what creates the *compound effect* of success. (Life lesson #10 as we discussed earlier, in case some of you forgot!).

8

GIP-Equis

Testing the Waters in India and Sowing the Seeds for Bimtek

A WISE MAN ONCE TOLD ME THAT IT TAKES AT LEAST FIVE years, if not more, to build a business from scratch. I had my fair share of entrepreneurial experiences in my early days, and after spending time in banking and private equity across regions, I believed I still had it in me to dedicate the next few years of my life to building the next chapter of my work journey.

I wanted to build a business from scratch—with a vision, a bigger purpose and a desire to do the right thing, with a DNA of *values over value*. It needed to be rooted in the learnings passed on by my parents and the desire to build their legacy.

Starting from zero and building a path to one is a challenge. Scaling from one to ten is a completely different challenge. I had experienced the former in my twenties while working on my start-up, but now, building something with a sizeable capital pool from the outset—an institutional setup driven by corporate governance, culture, values and people—was a task cut out before me at a significantly bigger scale.

The hunger and desire to build Bimtek the right way often kept me awake at night. I wanted it to be a venture with the right set of values, culture, mindset and the ability to create holistic value. Challenges naturally come with building any business, but in an emerging, developing market like India, these include softer, nuanced challenges very different from those one faces in a developed market such as the UK, or while sitting on an institutional desk at Morgan Stanley.

I believe my generation has had its basic necessities taken care of (per Maslow's hierarchy), and so the aspirations and desires of boomers and early millennials are in stark contrast to those of late millennials and Gen X, Z and beyond. The latter seek to build fast and see results even faster. Where earlier it would take decades to scale to billion-dollar revenues, now many businesses chase billion-dollar *valuations* in just a few short years.

Coming from an old-school mindset, I appreciated that building a business the *right* way would take time, especially if I wanted to do it with the right people, culture and values. To build something that lasts generations; to build something that, decades later, gives one a sense of contentment. A legacy: not mine, but my parents'. This was, is and always will be for them, the 'Bimtek' of my life. For my father, the man to whom I owe most of my learnings. Lessons that had been with me since an early age, but which I fully appreciated only later—whether validated at scale in institutional setups such as Goldman and Morgan Stanley, or when echoed in the principles, conduct and demeanour of investment greats like Warren Buffett, Charlie Munger, Peter Lynch and Howard Marks.

Thus began the transition from Morgan Stanley to Global Infrastructure Partners (GIP)–Equis in their India offices, in an advisory capacity, while simultaneously going back to the drawing board to articulate my vision, working plan and the building blocks for Bimtek. The idea was to gain experience with an institutional setup rooted in Indian DNA but operating at a global level, and to learn from some of the finest investment managers in Indian capital markets.

One of them was Ashutosh Sharma, then India Head of GIP–Equis. He is a gem of a person, with humility at his core and the requisite street smarts to build and manage a business in India. From spending time with Ash and the team, diligencing opportunities and day-to-day challenges in building a billion-dollar investment platform from scratch, the learnings were immense.

The premise of working at GIP–Equis was twofold: first, to help incubate a multi-billion-dollar investment platform from the ground up; second, to understand the back-end mechanics, operational semantics and on-ground execution at scale. The inferences from both were critical in forming the foundation for an institutional investment office in India.

On the first, we started with detailed desktop research on potential opportunities, progressing to internal 'preliminary investment screening memo' and built a financial model to evaluate the scope and feasibility of the opportunity.

Thereafter what followed was the deep diving and cold-towelling of every minute assumption of the investment underwrite by leveraging our own capabilities and those of external advisors, consultants, lawyers, investment bankers and subject matter experts, as well as the fund's investment team across the board. The preliminary go/no-go decision of the investment committee was then sought to commit a budget for deeper due diligence: testing the thesis, refining scale and structure and finalising sources and uses of funds at a monthly granularity.

After extensive diligence and ground-level engagement with business owners—validating the thesis, gauging interest and building a pipeline of similar opportunities—the investment committee sign-off was sought for the seed investment and, with it, the incubation of a new platform. After that we put together a dedicated team and operational set-up with a secured pipeline and path to grow the platform to the stipulated scale and size, setting up daily, weekly, monthly, quarterly and annual MIS (Management Information Systems) around it to capture every asset-level detail at the investment desk.

It was a near-assembly line of operational precision. Overall, the investment team's work on this seed asset opportunity spanned across the operations and portfolio management teams, on-ground execution and supervision through contractors, sub-contractors, consultants and lawyers, converging into coherent MIS built for investment committee-level reporting.

Ultimately, the ongoing execution, asset and management over a hold period ranging from five to seven years led to potential exit opportunities, either through IPOs, secondary sale to a private equity or a strategic investor. Setting up and ensuring the smooth running of this Optimus Prime kind of operational giant with cogwheels was where the devil lay—in the details!

Sitting in a fancy office building and leveraging our brain cells, as well as of those with decades of investing experience, is one thing, and probably one of the most important things for an investment by an investment fund, albeit operations is the key to success in any business. The real key lies in *execution*.

For instance, in real estate private equity or infrastructure funds, investment teams incubate platforms, but unless they understand on-ground execution, they risk being handcuffed by the operational teams' capabilities and their guesstimate of what's under control and how. The real differentiator is knowing the granular details: site master plans, material grades, bill of quantities, design specs, project management and the overall execution plan.

This was not just a challenge but an amazing experience for the work-obsessed and detail-oriented person that I have become over the years, or as someone who wouldn't be able to sleep at peace at night unless he's fully on top of everything going on in the scope of work, be it the financial model on Excel and the output numbers to six decimal points in terms of the IRR/returns as well as the operational execution plan.

Equally important was learning the investor relations and fundraising side. All of it was enjoyable: Meeting limited partners (LPs), taking them on asset tours to the actual site, socialising with them and educating them on investment thesis, ongoing investments, pipelines and potential fundraising efforts with existing and new LPs.

It was this trio—the **investment side**, the **operational side** and the **fundraising side**—that I worked across, end-to-end, at scale in a multi-billion-dollar fund house, that gave me the confidence, practice and readiness to execute the same playbook at my own firm, Bimtek.

With this overall machine put together as a process, I spent time across some of these specific investment avenues both on existing growth platforms, such as the one in the Indian renewable energy sector across solar, wind, hydro and thermal energy, and in evaluating and incubating other potential investment platforms across social infrastructure, such as hospitals, K-12 schools under a sale-leaseback model or highway roads on a toll-operate-transfer model or other industrial, warehousing asset opportunities.

Synergies from some of these platforms would eventually feed as directly transferable inputs for the Bimtek family office's infrastructure and warehousing platform. The fund house's head and my dear friend, Ashutosh, also sits on the advisory board and LP Advisory Committee of Bimtek Capital today, playing a pivotal role in shaping our corporate governance and acting as a sounding board across our endeavours.

9

Breaking the Box

Aspirations, Hunger and Drive to be the Best at What We Do

THE BHAGAVAT GITA SAYS THAT ONE SHOULD FOCUS ON THE tasks at hand and not on the end results. Eventually, things align with the bigger plan laid out for us by the higher power.

As much as I am a man of science and reasoning, I do believe in the concept of energies, the Yin and Yang of the world, and in the existence of a higher power, the 'God soul'. There is the belief system that our souls are immortal, transcending into different forms of life as we shift from one human form to another living being, until eventual liberation (*moksha*) is attained. In that lies the purpose of our lives, the path to enlightenment and liberation.

As a child, I used to watch the Indian TV series *Shaktimaan*, which aired on national television in the 1990s. *Shaktimaan* attained a higher state in life on the basis of meditation and the five elements of nature—air, water, fire, space and earth. A parallel could be drawn to the English cartoon series *Captain Planet*. I still recall the theme song that played before every episode and its lyrics in Hindi:

Hota hai jab aadmi ko apna gyaan, kehlaya wo shaktiman
Ye aatmik-shakti hai, duniya badal sakti hai
(When a person realises the true purpose of his existence, he attains enlightenment.)

At the time, I barely paid attention to these words. But years later, when this tune randomly crossed my mind and I found myself humming it, its depth struck me. The simplicity with which the path to enlightenment and purpose of life was expressed blew me away. After all, this is what Gautama Buddha realised when he attained enlightenment while meditating under the Bodhi tree—that a man attains enlightenment when he knows and learns about himself and the purpose of his existence.

As I mentioned earlier, my personal ikigai lies at the intersection of creating value for the broader ecosystem, the people who matter to me and myself, by working in the field of finance and making an impact with capital. On this path, I have chosen to remain rational while respecting the laws of nature, and by extension the higher power, whatever form or formlessness one chooses to see it in.

Thus, I am a firm believer that we should wholeheartedly pursue what we wish and on a *best effort basis*, without regrets—and ultimately surrender to the will of the higher power. This is consistent with teachings across faiths. For me, this is the point at which all religions and faiths converge into one spiritual sense.

This thought process also resonates with the Hindi saying: *'Chinta nahi, chintan karo.'* Instead of worrying (*chinta*) about problems outside our control, we should focus on what's under our control or the task at hand and leave the rest to the higher power through contemplation, prayer and reflection (*chintan*), staying centred and aligning ourselves to godliness, while walking the path towards enlightenment.

Only a few of us are fortunate enough to stumble upon or consciously discover our ikigai. Even fewer manage to implement it meaningfully in our lives. Personally, I spent a great deal of time pondering mine, sometimes brainstorming, literally writing on walls, figuring out what I enjoy, what I am good at, what made commercial sense in the world and what the world actually needed.

Separating these aspects and jotting down a list of each, then seeking potential areas of synergy and overlap, is by far the most practical way to figure out one's ikigai. But of course, it's easier said than done.

What has helped me most is the simple practice of occasionally pausing and reassessing my progress, asking myself what I am doing, how far I've come and whether I'm channelling my energy into the right pursuits. If not, the pause provides a chance to regroup and redirect.

This practice of *pause and reassess* has worked wonders for me, and I believe it can be an ongoing exercise for anyone seeking to define their ikigai.

Setting the Stage Around Bimtek: Parents and Their Legacy

Moving back to India and starting to work on my investment office, Bimtek Group, marks the second innings of my entrepreneurial journey. It was driven by the aspiration and desire to create an institutional investment office in India for the world.

I briefly touched on this when outlining the vision, working plan and building blocks of Bimtek during my time at GIP–Equis. However, what I want to speak about here are the core learnings rooted in the two pillars of Bimtek, my parents: Bim (from Bimla Chawla) and Tek (from Tek Chand Chawla).

These fundamental lessons are what we at Bimtek strive to leverage in our core conduct, culture and philosophy, centred on 'ideas, people and capital' and ensuring we focus on *values over value* across all our business ventures.

My Father: Tek Chand Chawla

The more time I have spent away from my father and family these past two decades or so, the more I have realised how the building blocks, the attitude, the mindset and the learnings that I have picked up along the way from some of the best people in their respective fields of work is nothing but an amalgamation of all the sanskaars and lessons that I have seen and come to realise from my father.

There's a song from a Bollywood movie that goes, '*Jag ghumeya ve, thaare jaesa na koi*' (I have travelled the world but haven't found anyone like you). The song is about a lover's admiration for their partner, but for me, it perfectly captures the sentiment of my admiration for my father and the lifelong validation of the lessons I learnt from him.

It is this feeling of awe, that after travelling the world and learning from the best, I realised everything was already there at home, with and through my father, and I thus appreciated the sheer luck of having being born to the right parents in the right family. It reinforced my belief that perhaps there is a plan for all of us.

Almost every child idolises their father. But as children grow up, it's natural to start seeing flaws in the older generation and differences in values and approaches between their parents and themselves. This often leads to a gradual, sometimes significant, reduction in the internal compass of respect.

The opposite has been true for me. Over the years, my respect and admiration for my father has only deepened. I have come to appreciate how he conducts himself personally with family and others, and how, despite starting from scratch, he built a business and grew it to the scale it is today.

He is an embodiment of the values of Maryada Purushottam Ram, a person who lives the qualities of the Hindu God Ram and the lessons his life imparts.

I joke with my family that most of my life will likely be spent institutionalising the family office setup while building businesses from scratch, driven by values and long-term-thinking, essentially carrying forward the legacy of my father. To him, I owe the greatest part of my learnings and accomplishments so far, and likely all that will come in the future.

My Mother: Bimla Chawla

Maavan thandiyaan chavaan.

As controversial as it may sound, a child may be the ugliest kid around, yet every mother loves her child unconditionally and tells her child she is the prettiest girl or the most handsome boy. It is only when one steps into the outside world that one truly begins to appreciate others' and, by extension, one's own physical appearance and character. No wonder mothers' love is considered the purest form of love.

I am grateful to mine for the absence of any sort of pressure or expectations and for her presence, which brings me peace and a feeling of pure bliss.

Most of us are fortunate to be blessed with parents, to live with them and to learn from them during our formative years. Some, unfortunately, do not have this blessing or are unable to spend enough time with their parents due to circumstances beyond their control.

Most religions teach that God resides within us and that serving one's parents is the true wealth in life. Yet, none explicitly state that God is physically embodied in our parents and that their blessings are the low-hanging fruit capable of swaying the world in our favour.

I am no Shravan Kumar—the boy who carried his blind parents in baskets tied to bamboo sticks and was accidentally killed by King Dashrath, Lord Ram's father, when the king mistook him for an animal drinking water at a lake in the forest. Upon hearing the tragic news, the boy's parents cursed King Dashrath to die painfully from separation from his own children—the poignant prelude to Lord Ram's exile and King Dashrath's demise in his absence.

That said, I strongly believe that whatever I have accomplished in life is due primarily to the grace of a higher power, my parents' blessings and perhaps a bit of luck—most likely in that order. It is fitting, then, that my life's work centres on building their legacy.

10

The Second Innings: Bimtek

A Vision. A Dream. Entrepreneurial Journey 2.0

The transition from working with GIP–Equis to the eventual launch of Bimtek Group occurred in 2019. Bimtek Group is an investment office focused on real estate and other alternative investments; that is, investments in the capital markets across public and private equities (listed and unlisted), debt and venture capital.

Bimtek's philosophy centres on 'ideas, people and capital'. Fundamentally, it is about doing the right thing and prioritising values over value. We leverage our human and intellectual capabilities to create value for the broader ecosystem and our stakeholders, responsibly, and in the financial sense on a risk-adjusted returns basis.

At Bimtek, we strongly believe that our people, ideas and alignment of interests with our investor base, that is, our own proprietary capital invested alongside investors' funds, drives the Bimtek advantage.

The fundamental idea behind Bimtek Group is to leverage our network across financial institutions and diverse capital pools, both domestic and international, combined with our money management skills, to build a values-driven institution, which is able to help resolve on-ground challenges in India whilst creating value for all stakeholders.

Leveraging our Ikigai: Skills, Learnings, Opportunity and Capabilities to Create Value for the Ecosystem, Nation and Self

Personally, having had the opportunity to work with and learn from some of the best people across various industries, geographies and cultural mindsets, it made logical sense for me to establish an institutional office where we could leverage our network, resources, capabilities and skillset to create value for all.

India is currently in a sweet spot for growth over the coming decades, fuelled by favourable demographics, increasing formalisation and digitisation of the economy. Yet, it faces obvious on-ground challenges that, if solved, could catalyse India becoming the epicentre of global growth for years to come.

To my mind, *healthcare, education and infrastructure* are the three most important pillars of holistic growth in any economy. Ironically, these are also the areas where India still faces substantial challenges and requires significant catch-up compared to other global economies. Coincidentally, two of these three sectors align with Bimtek's and my areas of expertise.

China, for example, has grown leaps and bounds compared to India over the past decades simply by focusing on these big-ticket problems. This focus has not only catalysed China's growth but also provided its population better access to value creation. They now have access to a high quality of life instead of being stuck in traffic jams or struggling to access quality education and infrastructure.

Emulating these basic yet critical capabilities presents massive growth and value-unlocking opportunities for India.

Take logistics, for instance: its costs as a percentage of India's GDP are among the highest worldwide, around 8–10 per cent, compared to a global standard of 3–5 per cent. This implies a potential savings opportunity of 5–7 per cent of GDP annually if inefficiencies in logistics, supply chain and warehousing across the Indian ecosystem can be resolved.

This premise underpins Bimtek's warehousing platform, Indus Global Industrial Spaces (IGIS), launched with the vision of creating world-class warehousing facilities and technology-enabled logistics parks across India.

On the education front, there are two key avenues: access to information or education and quality of education. Fortunately, India has addressed the primary facet in the past decade by making access to primary education free for all children. The deeper challenge remains in the *quality* of education and the learning experience in both private and state institutions, as well as in the overall curriculum and pedagogy during the formative years, from K-12 through higher education.

Despite studying at India's premier engineering institution, the IIT, it pains me to say that India's education ecosystem still has a long way to go. But instead of only complaining, at Bimtek we have aspired to set up higher education institutions with curricula that are more practical, industry-oriented and skills-driven, run and led by professionals from diverse industries rather than the prevalent *textbook-style* theoretical approach.

Bimtek's investment arm, Bimtek Capital, is also evaluating partnerships with some of India's best K-12 school chains. The aim is to provide capital access to promoters who have cracked the code for delivering quality education, enabling them to focus on what they do best—imparting quality education—and, with strategic financial investors' backing, to grow and scale. This fulfils our aspiration to create value for the education ecosystem, the institutions, our stakeholders and ourselves.

Regarding healthcare, despite internal debates and ideas at Bimtek, our current focus remains on building the education and logistics platforms, placing *direct* healthcare problem-solving on the back burner due to capacity constraints. However, we have identified some promising players in healthcare institutions, diagnostics and the healthcare-pharmaceutical supply chain who are addressing primary issues in India's healthcare ecosystem. We have backed some of these through financial exposure—capital injection or indirect ownership—via Bimtek Capital's India Growth Fund.

Brief Synopsis of Bimtek Capital's India Growth Fund

Being long-term bullish on the India growth story was the basis and genesis of my decision to move back to India in 2019 and set up Bimtek here, and not in a fancy office in London, New York or Dubai.

We identified sectors and segments of value creation in India that lie at the intersection of our competence and understanding and are run by management teams that are prudent capital allocators while being focused on sustainable value creation. We thereby launched Bimtek Capital's India Growth Fund.

Initially, we tested the thesis with our own proprietary capital, and more recently with capital from friends and extended family. We are now on the path to institutionalisation, moving towards managing institutional monies.

The journey of Bimtek Capital's India Growth Fund officially began in 2019, when we put together a portfolio of companies with a medium-to-long-term holding period, attractively positioned to capture massive tailwinds in the Indian economy. These tailwinds and megatrends include the financialisation of India's savings (higher incremental allocation and rebalancing of household savings towards financial assets such as direct equities, debt and mutual funds, versus traditional saving avenues such as gold and real estate), digitisation of the economy, ease of doing business and a shift from offline to omnichannel distribution.

These megatrends have been ridden like waves by a select few leading businesses in various industries, where the market is not winner-take-all, but is dominated by a handful of winners.

Amid structural shifts taking place in India, such as the formalisation of the economy, equity penetration of savings, the entry of 100–150 million young people into the workforce annually and healthy projected GDP growth, Bimtek believes India has a long runway for growth.

Currently, we stand at an inflection point: India's per capita income is set to grow significantly, putting us on a trajectory that mirrors China's position a decade or two ago. The *Economist*, in its 2022/23 editorial, rightly states: '… a novel confluence of forces stands to transform India's economy over the next decade, improving the lives of 1.4 billion people and changing the balance of power in Asia … As the country emerges from the pandemic, however, a new pattern of growth is visible. It is unlike anything you have seen before. These changes help explain why *India* is forecast to be the world's fastest-growing big economy and why it has a chance of holding on to that title for years ...'*

India is going through a phase similar to the US in the late nineteenth and early twentieth centuries, when the economy was networked with the emergence of railroads, telegraph, cars and roads. Massive improvements in transport and communication networks, banking systems, tax regimes and social security distribution via Jan Dhan bank accounts (J), the national identity and social security system Aadhaar (A) and cheap access to internet and mobile connectivity (M) (JAM) are enabling efficient, well-capitalised companies with competitive advantages to consolidate entire industries. This is evident in the shift from informal to formal and offline to online, and their growing market share. The Indian economy's growth and prosperity will create immense value for the national ecosystem, businesses and entrepreneurs.

At Bimtek, our philosophy is simple: ride these megatrends while staying vigilant to avoid dubious businesses. Our approach aligns with the ideology of 'growth at a reasonable price'. Being the boring value investors that we are, we keep a strong hold on the *value* of the business and in sectors we understand with strong long-term tailwinds. We buy into these businesses at significant discounts to our estimates of fundamental value (that is, purchase price paid being much less than value), thereby generating outsized returns as the market recognises their worth. Simply put, it's like buying the latest $1,000 iPhone for $500–700. Yes, such undervaluation happens—in markets swayed by

---

* 'The Indian economy is being rewired. The opportunity is immense', *The Economist*, 13 May 2022, https://www.economist.com/leaders/2022/05/13/the-indian-economy-is-being-rewired-the-opportunity-is-immense.

greed and fear, where securities frequently trade at deep discounts to or even multiple times their fair value.

Bimtek's USP lies in identifying gold-standard businesses trading at discounted prices with strong growth prospects in the years ahead, so we can generate significant returns over a three to five-year or longer investment holding period and thus make healthy returns overall, while taking minimal risk or making superior risk-adjusted returns.

Bimtek Real Estate and Infrastructure Platform

The Bimtek Real Estate and Infrastructure platform has been envisaged and built upon the foundation my father laid in real estate, as well as expanded to encompass investments in real estate and broader infrastructure that address India-specific problems within our core competency areas.

Earlier, we discussed the fundamental premise of challenges in India, and how at Bimtek, we are leveraging our capabilities to solve these India-specific issues through key identified areas of value creation: education, infrastructure and healthcare.

Focusing on infrastructure, Bimtek's warehousing platform, Indus Global Industrial Spaces (IGIS), was incubated with the vision to develop world-class Grade-A warehousing facilities and technology-enabled logistics parks across India, aimed at streamlining and reducing logistics costs. For example, our seed asset is a million square feet of Grade-A warehousing space across a logistics park in Delhi NCR, with a secured pipeline of similar assets across North India for the initial phase and expansion planned across tier-1 cities.

On the real estate side, the existing portfolio of residential and commercial spaces serves as a cash cow supporting the more enterprising avenues of capital allocation. These include core areas such as Bimtek Capital and the IGIS warehousing platform, as well as growth avenues through broader capital market endeavours. In venture capital, we invest in and support the growth of businesses that are solving real problems on the ground in India, particularly in the consumer technology space.

11

Putting Together the Right Building Blocks of Success in Professional and Personal Life

Over the years, I have come to realise how the compound effect of some basic building blocks in our day-to-day lives can have an outsized impact on outcomes, both personally and professionally. Here, I share these insights through anecdotal references, stories and life lessons.

It's like in finance, where we rely on rules and checklists—ticking off potential risk factors during investment due diligence and exploring ways to mitigate them, all to achieve the best risk-adjusted return and create an air-tight investment underwrite. Similarly, in life, I have realised that simple daily activities and our conduct can have a tremendous, outsized effect on results.

I am not a big fan of self-help books, and would rather draw lessons from my own experiences, both successes and failures.

However, every now and then, I have skimmed through some bestsellers to check if I'm missing something obvious, only to realise that many of the fundamental building blocks we discuss here form the essence and backbone of those books as well.

Equanimity in Life: A Balanced, Centred State

It is common wisdom that time never remains the same for anyone. It changes, be it the four seasons or the phases in life, whether good or bad. It's an obvious fact that life throws challenges and curveballs at each of us every now and then. What matters most is not giving in, but persevering with equanimity, peace and a centred state of mind, using the small progress made each day to create a snowball effect.

The metaphor of the snowball, gradually adding volume and gaining in size and momentum as it rolls downhill, illustrates the catalytic power of consistent effort and discipline in life, compounding to create outsized returns.

Even Lord Ram endured exile when his stepmother, Kaikeyi, invoked a promise from his father, King Dashrath, asking him to send Ram to the forest for fourteen years and crown her own son Bharat as king in his place. This request had to be fulfilled to honour a vow King Dashrath made years earlier to grant two wishes to Kaikeyi in repayment for saving his life during a difficult time. Being a man of his word and true character, Lord Ram accepted his father's wish without question and went into exile with his wife Sita, accompanied by his younger brother Laxman. During exile, Ram faced numerous trials, including the abduction of Sita by Ravana. Fourteen years later, he returned to Ayodhya and was crowned king, while his younger brother Bharat ruled as regent during his absence, acting as caretaker in Ram's name rather than becoming king himself.

This story offers many lessons: about honouring one's word, relationships, depth of character, self-sacrifice and loyalty. It shows King Dashrath's unwavering commitment to his promise, Lord Ram's unquestioning obedience and Bharat's sacrifice in forgoing power, awaiting Ram's rightful return.

Life Lesson #16: Equanimity in life. Let it flow; come to you.

Depth of Character: Lord Ram's Precedent

All through my life, I have admired Lord Ram and studied his character through the *Ramcharitramanas*, a book that describes his life and lessons. To my mind, he's the perfect son, the perfect student, the perfect brother, the perfect ruler and so much more. Was he a near-perfect husband too? I might have a slightly controversial opinion on this.

There's an incident in the Ramayana, as per Hindu mythology, where one evening Lord Ram, dressed to disguise himself as a common man, went around his kingdom to observe the state of affairs. During this exercise, he overheard a man arguing with his wife, complaining that he was not as accepting as Ram and could never live with a wife who had allegedly spent time with another man.

Subsequently, Lord Ram questioned his wife Sita in his courtroom about her time in captivity by Ravana. Sita affirmed that despite her captivity, she had no relation with Ravana. Lord Ram did not believe her, and legend has it that Sita then prayed to the Goddess of Earth to end her life if she were not telling the truth. The Goddess of Earth affirmed Sita's truthfulness and eventually took Sita away with her.

Maybe this is where I believe Lord Ram could have been slightly different as a trusting husband, not relying on the judgement of one of his subjects. But I am no one to opine on him.

Regardless, Lord Ram is revered because he exemplified how one can maintain inner peace, balance and equanimity despite life's trials and tribulations.

I have tried to be directionally guided by the *Ramcharitmanas* and Lord Ram's embodiment of character to be a better son to my parents, a better brother to my siblings, a better partner to my lady, hopefully a better parent when the time comes, a better friend to my near and dear ones and ultimately a better human being for society at large.

Life Lesson 17: Do the right thing. Be kind, generous and compassionate. Prioritise values over value.

Every person's life is influenced by the people they spend the most time with. There's a saying that we become a mixture of the characteristics of the five people we spend the most time with. There does seem to be merit in how our ideologies and thought processes are impacted by those around us, either directly or subconsciously, especially when our views differ from theirs.

In my personal life, my parents and my partner have played a pivotal role. My father has always told me, since childhood, that the test of a man's character is his faithfulness to his word. There's a Hindi saying: '*Ram se bada Ram ka naam*', meaning God's name holds more power than God himself. For context, in the Ramayana, there is an incident where the *vanar sena* (monkey army), led by Sugriv, was marching towards Sri Lanka to fight Ravana's army and rescue Sita. They reached the Indian Ocean and struggled to find a way to cross. Lord Ram, sitting in disappointment on the shore, was having a think while absentmindedly throwing small stones into the sea. Lord Hanuman, seeing what he was doing, started doing the same, but he wrote 'Ram' on every stone before throwing it. To everyone's surprise, the stones floated. Soon, the entire monkey army was writing 'Ram' on rocks and throwing them into the water, and this is how they built, with stones, a bridge to cross the ocean and reach Sri Lanka.

Lord Ram defeated Ravana and rescued Sita, a victory celebrated across India as Dusshera, followed by Diwali, the festival of lights, a few days later, marking Lord Ram's return to Ayodhya.

Scientists have researched and validated the evidence of this bridge, and most recently, the Bollywood movie *Ram Setu* (The Bridge of Ram) dramatised the story. The point: there is more strength in God's name than God himself. By extension, a man of his word is worth more than anything else.

One of America's wisest men, Warren Buffett, is often quoted as saying: 'A man's reputation precedes him.' This is echoed in corporate finance, where the *integrity of the management team* is often cited as the single most important factor in a business's success, besides the underlying business model.

Thus the lifelong lesson: remain true to your word and commitments, regardless of outcomes, even if it means taking a hit, monetary or otherwise.

Realisation: What You Seek Is Seeking You!

Even though I am not a big fan of Bollywood movies or Shah Rukh Khan, who's practically treated as demi-god by the public, let me borrow a clichéd quote from one of Shah Rukh's movies:

*'Kisi cheez ko agar tum shiddat se chaaho toh saari kainaat
tumhe usse milane mein lag jaati hai.'*
(If you seek something with all your heart and dedication,
then the whole universe conspires to help you achieve it.)

In life, when we chase happiness, it eludes us, but when we
start focusing on what's within our control, what we can act on
consistently, that is when happiness itself arrives. It settles on us
like the gentle breeze that caresses the face when we stand out in
the open, whether in the countryside or mountains. That's when
the world aligns to make things happen for us.

Physically Fit. Mentally Alert. Morally Straight.

My association with the Bharat Scouts and Guides mission
during my high school years taught me a wide range of life
skills—camping, knotting and estimation, general safety and
self-defence, disaster preparedness and management and how to
contribute meaningfully to society.

The motto of the mission has stayed with me and resonates
strongly with my mindset: 'Physically fit. Mentally alert. Morally
straight.'

I started working out in my late teens and early twenties as
a college kid inspired by movie actors with bulky physiques and
abs, wanting that body for myself too. *Solah ka dola*, as the Punjabi
saying goes—sixteen-inch biceps—by going to the gym, working
out, eating well and gulping down protein shakes. That partially
happened for me by building the right body frame: shoulders,
back and biceps, that is, the upper body structure. Abs, not so
much. It wasn't a failed attempt; it was a naïve attempt focused
on aesthetics.

Over the past seven to ten years, I've shifted to eating healthy, working out briefly three to four times a week, running in the park a couple of times, respecting my body with rest, good sleep and meditation, a practice I've maintained for over two decades. Because of the compound effect of these habits, I've started feeling much happier, more at peace with my body and thoughts (mind) and having a general sense of well-being. Working out has become an integral part of my life to the point that I sometimes feel off on the few days I don't exercise or meditate.

Besides building stamina, grit and determination through fitness, working out has reinforced the *habit of sticking through when things get difficult, going through the grind and finishing what I started.*

Playing football as a kid helped me develop my running, but I've only recently come to truly appreciate the 'runner's high', the adrenaline and the significant rise in my happiness quotient. Hollywood actor Will Smith, during his Academy Awards acceptance speech a few years ago, rightly captured the essence of running: when your heart pounds, feeling like it might explode and you want to give up, that's precisely when you should push forward instead of quitting. It's about not giving up when it's the hardest. Starting something, following through and most importantly, finishing it. That is what builds depth of character and perseverance.

I often draw a silly parallel in my head: when I am struggling with something, I try cooking two-minute noodles. The sense of accomplishment that comes from starting, doing and finishing—even something so simple—is borderline lame, but these small victories sometimes keep us going in tricky times.

Counting Blessings and Being Grateful

Doing good for anyone and everyone without expecting anything in return and being morally straight as a person has worked well for most people.

In India, post-Independence, our grandparents' generation primarily focused on building basic necessities as per Maslow's hierarchy of needs—food, clothing, shelter—given that by the time of Independence in 1947, the British had looted India of much of its wealth and prosperity. No wonder the Indian movies of the 1960s and 1970s often centred on these themes, with titles like *Roti, Kapda Aur Makaan* reflecting societal concerns. For movies are primarily a reflection of the society.

Our parents' generation grew up with access to these basic necessities, enabling them to pursue education and better lives through employment in national and multinational corporations, especially after the liberalisation and globalisation reforms introduced in the 1990s by then-Finance Minister Dr Manmohan Singh. Some became first- or second-generation entrepreneurs.

Now, our third generation post-Independence has broadened the definition of life's basics to include education alongside food, clothing and shelter. Our generation has expressed itself through professional endeavours across arts, religion, science, research, medicine and entrepreneurship, among others.

We are all born with certain privileges. Anyone whose basic needs are met is born privileged, whether they acknowledge it or not. The degree of prosperity may vary from lower- or middle-income groups to wealthy households, but everyone on this spectrum has been blessed with basic privileges to be grateful for. Despite global development, many in the world are still born into poverty; about five million children die annually due to lack of access to basic healthcare. Even a minor injury to a finger disrupts our daily life, making it hard to eat properly, write or conduct oneself as desired. Consider those living with physical handicaps, who face life's basic and daily endeavours with grit and determination.

It's these little things in life that allow us to appreciate what we have, what we were born with and where we aspire to be. So it's good to take a step back and appreciate the sheer luck of being born the way we are and whatever circumstantial set-up we are born into. Thus, we should be grateful for what we have and not complain about the lack of things, resources or access if we are among the ones born with these basic privileges. It's this attitude that lets the mind appreciate what we have, our present and what we aspire to be and achieve and thus shapes the path we follow to get there.

For example, I was born into a comfortable family; everything was taken care of, more than one could ask for. With this background, and by understanding my father's character and journey, the benchmark has been set so high that I grew up with the insecurity as to whether my own children will respect me as much as I respect and look up to my father.

Being born with privileges or a 'silver spoon' is one thing; appreciating that position and then building something of our own, using our own capabilities, charting our own path instead of living in predecessors' shadows or wasting opportunities, is another. This desire to do something credible in life and independent of the family name has fuelled me each day—with passion, sheer desire and purpose.

Whether waking up at 4 a.m. in my teenage years to meditate and study for the IIT entrance exams; starting my own venture in my twenties; going to study at the best business schools of the world, slogging 16–18-hour workdays at Goldman Sachs and

Morgan Stanley; or now working on my second entrepreneurial journey in setting up an institutional investment office—this drive persists.

The vision of looking back thirty years from now, feeling content about having built something meaningful for myself, my loved ones and the broader ecosystem while adhering to the core values learned from my parents, i.e., 'values over value', is what wakes me up and drives me daily. The hope that my children might one day look up to me, even in part, as I do to my father, his conduct and accomplishments, is a catalyst too.

Thus, the daily note-to-self in the expression of gratitude—to God, for health, life and what we have, and for the happiness of ourselves, our loved ones and those around us.

I have maintained a journal for over a decade now. It is not limited to gratitude, but captures my state of mind, thought processes at that particular point, what I have been doing and occasionally reflecting back to review the depth of my thinking from a few years back and self-learning, evolution journey.

Habits and Discipline

Just as chaos theory teaches us that a few small changes at the beginning can have a massive impact (delta) on the final outcome, similarly, the atomic habits, or the small changes, we make in our day-to-day lives bring order to the chaos around us.

Almost all of us learnt about compounding in high school mathematics. Its application in life? Not many did. It took me some time to appreciate the power of compounding in life, but once it settled in my thought process, it changed my perspective and, by extension, my life.

The boring and 'not so sexy' stuff is where the magic happens. That's where the compounding effect of consistency plays out.

The outsized returns or the supposed 'overnight' success happens here. I can't emphasise this enough! I hear this echoed by so many successful people around the world, who follow a process and stick to an almost borderline boring routine day in and day out—whether for exercise, fitness, work, or anything they set out to achieve.

Personally, I apply a cheat code in my life: where, in case I struggle to concentrate or work, as we all do sometimes, instead of giving up for the day, I pick the easiest task I can finish by applying myself. Be it a quick skim through an investment memo, responding to emails or ticking off trivial tasks from my daily to-do list. This reinforces my thought process that I am back on track doing something meaningful.

Again: *Starting something. Doing it. And finishing it!*

This process creates a self-reinforcing positive cycle, where transitioning to the next task at hand doesn't feel hectic and the day proceeds as it ideally should or on a similar basis. It's these little things that build determination and perseverance, reminding us that even on our worst days, we went through the grind, got things done and got closer to what we set out to acheive—one small step at a time. Or simply accomplishing something and doing something incremental on days we don't feel like getting out of bed.

One point at a time. One game at a time. One set at a time. One match at a time.

This is to paraphrase the words of arguably the greatest tennis player the world has ever seen, yes, Roger Federer, on how he focuses on little tasks at hand instead of thinking too much about the outcome of the game, match or championship.

One does need the ability to zoom in and zoom out of situations, and have perspective on where we want to be, head towards it and course-correct when required. But it's staying present and focused on the task at hand on an ongoing basis that gets the ball rolling in the right direction.

Take Mahendra Singh Dhoni, the legendary Indian cricketer and captain, widely considered one of the best finishers in the game. His secret? In his own words, he focuses on taking the game deeper, one ball at a time, bringing it closer to the finish and flurries at the end, trusting his skill and ability to win the game for his team.

Networking: The Grunitzky Effect

During my time at HEC Paris School of Management, I learnt about the power of networking through the anecdotal reference to an African entrepreneur Claude Grunitzky. The founder and editor-in-chief of the lifestyle publication *TRACE*, an international fashion and music magazine, and co-founder of the TRACE TV network, Grunitzky comes from a humble background and could easily serve as one of the best case studies of hustle and networking in any business school curriculum.

Bumping into him and learning about his networking secret sauce directly from the horse's mouth was pure gold. Grunitzky maintains an Excel list of people he met over the years, classifying them by degree of connection—direct, acquaintances, introduced through a network, etc.—and by closeness of relationship, along with relevant contact details.

Over time, he built a powerful list of people across industries and disciplines, making an effort to keep in touch with them based on the warmth and comfort of his relationship with each one. Every time he faced an issue, needed a sounding board, wanted to test an idea or sought introductions, his Excel behemoth would reveal a few prospective leads worth reaching out to. Depending on his ongoing connection with them, he could extract value in the form of advice, input or introductions to people relevant for what he was seeking.

Grunitzky was essentially running an offline version of LinkedIn and Facebook merged into one, leveraging the compound effect of this network together with his own skills to catalyse his career. The genius of this compounding effect, and the impact he has made across the board, is fascinating, especially considering that he is now sought after by some of the most powerful and influential people in the world.

Negotiations and Creating Agreement

My time at HEC Paris was pivotal in the sense that some of the building blocks and inputs gathered there have stayed with me. In fact, there are certain portions of the curriculum that I have revisited over the past decade. The course on negotiations and creating agreement is one of them. Initially, it stayed with me as coursework, but over the years I have appreciated it more as a life skill. It was conducted by the late Mrs Nancy Caldwell, who had advised several high-profile CXOs across Europe and the US on some of their most important business deals, particularly on the softer aspects of negotiation.

As Nancy would often say, which has remained imprinted in my mind, it is always advisable to be prepared with one's BATNA and WATNA before entering a negotiation, BATNA being the *best alternative to a negotiated agreement* and WATNA the *worst alternative to a negotiated agreement.*

Equally important is to listen and absorb the other party's position and interests—namely, the underlying goals, interests they seek to fulfil in the negotiation. Asking the right questions to get these inputs allows us to differentiate between *interests* and *positions.* By extension, this enables us to practise the principle of *being hard on problems and soft on people*, and not the other way around, which most of us tend to do in both personal and professional discussions.

In most situations, there are ways to increase the size of the value pie and thereby find a mutually agreeable solution that carries more value than the base case for either party.

There is an old saying that a negotiation in which neither party leaves entirely happy is the ideal one, since each has compromised to arrive at an agreement. However, adopting the mindset of expanding the value pie for all parties involved can, in fact, lead to a better outcome for everyone, provided one remains cognisant of these softer aspects and the true interests at stake.

Reading and Writing

Charlie Munger (un)famously once said that he has never met a successful person who doesn't read a lot. It is also said that CXOs often end up reading 400–500 pages each day.

As a kid, the first time I learnt about the legendary investor Warren Buffett, I was surprised to discover that one of the richest men in the world simply sits and reads all day long in his office. All day. Most days. Consistently. His routine: head to the office, pick up breakfast at McDonald's on the way and then sit in his cabin reading for hours. He once even described himself as a 'book with hands, legs and a head'.

Each passing day in my own life has made me appreciate the genius of the man even more—how his eagerness and desire to learn daily, while consciously staying away from things he considered too difficult, whether in business or otherwise, shaped him. That consistency, sticking to his 'circle of competence', is what made him what he is and has been for decades, not just a money-making machine, but a knowledge powerhouse and a good man.

Books are a means of standing on the shoulders of giants, helping us foresee or resonate with their experiences and make our own lives easier, whether by learning from their successes or by avoiding their biggest mistakes.

Life Lesson #18: Importance of reading a lot and putting our thoughts down in writing.

Learn to Say No

Saying no is a skill very few possess. Most people struggle to say NO to things they ideally should turn down and end up spreading themselves too thin in terms of effort and time, which in turn dilutes their output. Simplifying life, both in terms of what we focus on achieving, as well as what we choose to do (and more importantly, what we choose *not* to do) on a daily basis is a key factor in determining where we eventually end up.

Stating the blindly obvious, but we live in a world of information overload. Everyone is connected to and aware of, much of what happens globally through constant access to information across platforms and devices. Setting aside the debate around misinformation, even in its purest form information overload can be overwhelming. In such a context, being deliberate about what we choose to focus on, and how, becomes just as important as how we conduct ourselves.

It reminds me of Indian cricketer Rahul Dravid's approach—leaving or defending the good deliveries, and only playing the bad ones to score runs. Over time, this discipline made him one of the most consistent players of the game, someone who stood tall in difficult situations and rightly earned the nickname 'The Wall'.

Warren Buffett once told a group of students at a school to view their lives as a punch card: each decision they make punches one slot, and since there are only a limited number of slots, they must be mindful of how they use them. We all face multiple decision trees in our day-to-day lives as well as when we make key decisions. That is why it becomes so important to say no to the things that hinder us from where we want to be in life and from achieving what we set out to accomplish.

Personally, I learnt this lesson very early in life. As a reluctant, strong-headed kid, clarity of thought and the ability to appreciate the power of saying no took its own sweet time to develop.

Along with my cousin brother, I would spend my summer holidays playing and learning cricket at the coaching academy run by the former captain of the Indian cricket team, Bishan Singh Bedi, held at the Jamia Milia Islamia Sports Grounds in Delhi. A driver would take us there every morning at 5:30 a.m. The day began with running ten full rounds of the cricket ground as a preliminary warm-up, followed by stretching and loosening exercises. Breakfast would be a glass of milk and bananas, after which we trained in the nets for a couple of hours, followed by a brief fifteen-over game, lunch and then winding up the day by 4 p.m. This was repeated six days a week for three months.

Most kids love sports—some love all sports, while some are drawn to just a few. Very few, however, develop strong feelings against one. I never knew I could dislike a game so much until that cricket camp, where I played so badly on purpose that people were left wondering if I had *any* skill at all. I would deliberately drop catches, field badly, bowl wides that would bisect the gap between the wicketkeeper and third man or get bowled out by the easiest deliveries while batting. I basically played as badly as possible, and intentionally so.

At the end of the camp, a felicitation ceremony was held, with Bishan Singh Bedi and Kapil Dev, another Indian cricketing legend and former team captain, handing out certificates and mementos. On stage, each kid was praised for a particular skill: someone's outswing bowling, another's cover drive or reverse swing. When my turn came, Kapil Dev shook my father's hand as well as mine, and the only comment Mr Bedi made about my skillset was that I was 'a bit on the naughtier side'.

My father, never a pushy parent, was puzzled. The first thing he asked me afterwards was, 'So, they didn't have even a single good thing to say about your game? How could someone be that bad at cricket or have no skill at all?'

Cricket for us in India is like football in Europe or baseball in the US. While hockey is our national sport, cricket reigns supreme, so much so that most children's first toy is a bat or a ball.

My response to him was simple: 'I don't like cricket at all! I want to play football.' It took me a full summer camp to gather the courage to say it out loud. Of course, I wouldn't say I never played cricket again. I still play once in a while with childhood friends, follow the game and admire many of its legends. But football has since become an integral part of my life.

The lesson? Learning to say no to what one doesn't enjoy and focusing instead on what one truly loves can be transformative. I learnt this the hard way, but early enough, and it has helped enormously since. I went on to play decent football through my school and college years, at district and state levels, and wherever I lived abroad, and still passionately follow and pride association with the sport for over two and a half decades now.

Life Lesson #19: The power of saying no—and simply focusing on the things one enjoys and aspires to—can compound into wonders in life.

As Warren Buffett puts it, *'The ability to say "no" is a tremendous advantage for an investor.'* For we come across numerous opportunities each day, but knowing which ones to pounce on—and which, in fact most, to leave—has a massive impact on outcomes.

My Attitude Towards Money

To my mind, anyone who claims money isn't important in life is either delusional or simply hypocritical. We often meet people who preach that money doesn't matter or that it cannot buy happiness. But what they fail to acknowledge is the confidence, sense of comfort and peace of mind that financial security provides, the freedom to spend time as one wishes: to pursue passions, do what we are good at and live on our own accord without constant worry. The list is long!

During the formative years of our career, it is far more important to focus on learning and gaining experience than on chasing the highest paycheque. To my mind, over the medium to long term, it all normalises. This resonates with an old saying in finance: the stock market is a voting machine in the short run, but a weighing scale in the long run. This essentially means that in the short term, the market is driven by investor sentiment and thus can exhibit irrationality, exuberance, fear or greed. But in the long term, it is driven by fundamentals: the market price eventually catches up with the underlying business performance.

Life behaves in much the same way. Without focusing solely on money, especially in the early years, if one works on building skills, knowledge and experience, the money inevitably follows. More often than not, this progress mirrors exponential growth—a hockey-stick curve—where the world celebrates it as 'overnight success'. But the truth is that behind every so-called overnight success lie years of hard work, honing of skills and persistence. The money comes as a by-product, not the goal itself.

> **Life Lesson #20:** Not running after money, but instead learning early on, ensures things fall into place, even financially.

12

Pivotal Impact—People and Life Incidents

Sometimes in life, nothing happens for decades and other times, decades happen in days.

Part of the Bigger Plan

I AM A STRONG BELIEVER THAT THROUGHOUT OUR LIFETIME, there are pivotal moments or people who guide the course of our lives so significantly that we only come to appreciate their impact when looking back. Perhaps it is part of a bigger plan for each of us.

In my case, I can count a few such instances of people entering my life or incidents occurring that have had a profound impact and likely changed the course of my life.

Paramhans Dayalji's Blessings

*Fall in love in such a way that it frees you from any connecting.
That's very different from the lonely wail of, 'she left me, he left
me; she came back; she left again'.*

—Rumi

The mind of a child is pure, as is their heart. As we gain worldly wisdom, this is no longer true. I have come to realise that people tend to be more God-fearing than God-loving. We see this every day, including in films, where people go to their respective places of worship—temples, mosques, churches—and 'ask' their gods for what they want.

I have often heard people preaching that if one does not perform certain deeds, something bad will happen. This is an indicator of a truly God-fearing mindset. Rarely do I come across people who exhibit genuine love for their version of God.

My sister Gunjan is an example of modern-day Meera Bai. Meera Bai was a Rajput queen who fell in love with Lord Krishna as a devoted follower, to the extent that she would lose all track of time while meditating or feel so deeply connected to Krishna's presence that she forgot everything happening around her.

Growing up in our home, we had a large pooja room (mandir) where my mom and dad performed aarti (prayer) every morning and evening without fail. I remember how each morning, when Gunjan woke up, she would come out of her room with her eyes shut, walk towards the pooja room, then open her eyes to do 'darshan'—she wanted to ensure that she saw the divine figures as the first sight of her day. She would smile, as if saying good morning to her loved ones, before going about her day. This purity of love stayed with me; the idea that the first face she wanted to see every morning was God's was a source of pure love and an inspiration for me.

As I mentioned earlier, my parents introduced me to Paramhans Dayalji and Shri Anandpur as a child. For some reason, it felt like home and peace every time I went to seek Paramhans Dayalji's blessings in Anandpur. My love for him ('Gurumaharaj ji', as we address him) has grown with every passing day since I first had the fortune of being in his gracious presence as a child.

Whether reading the holy book *Shri Granth* and learning from his life lessons and teachings, or spending time at Anandpur doing seva (selfless service) such as washing dishes, serving food, cleaning, attending morning and evening aarti, admiring his eternal and blissful presence, meditating, attending satsang kirtan (spiritual lessons) or simply keeping him in my heart wherever I was and whatever I was doing—his presence has been constant in my life.

On one fortunate occasion, Shri Gurumaharaj ji, in a blissful mood, said to me: '*Tum prabhu ke naam par toh wo tumhare kaam par. Tum apne kaam par toh prabhu apne dhaam par.*' ('If you keep God in your heart and being, then everything you seek will be taken care of.')

In 2017, Shri Paramhans Dayalji visited Bangalore, and I went to seek his blessings. My heart sank when I saw him that day. Shri Gurumaharaj ji was sitting in a wheelchair, pushed by Premi Mahatma ji, one of his disciples who stays with him most of the time, as he entered the prayer hall for the aarti pooja. Out of nowhere, I started crying—seeing him in such a tender state overwhelmed me completely. Although there were thousands of people in the hall, it felt as if my eyes had lost their sensory power of association with my brain and the physical sense of control, and I simply could not stop crying throughout the aarti and until he left the hall.

The mind cannot comprehend the matters of the heart.

Little did I know then that this would be the last time I would see him in his gracious physical presence. It felt like all the love in my heart was pouring out. I recall that moment vividly, and it still gives me goosebumps even as I write this.

Rumi's words come to mind:

It is good that the soul which had no true love ceased to exist,
Otherwise, it would be but shame.
Get drunk with love, love is all that exists;
Without the business of love, the beloved cannot be reached.

As it is rightly said, spiritual love is immortal; physical love is transitory. It is this love for the divine that sets us on the path to unification with a higher power and put us on the path to enlightenment.

I feel blessed to have been introduced to Shri Anandpur as a child, to have inculcated the habit of meditation in my early teens and to have continued on this path of spirituality and meditation every day to such an extent that it has now become part of my being.

I cannot imagine what my life would have been like, or how I would have been as a person, had I not embarked on this path to spiritual awakening and the effect it has had on everything in my life. There have been moments when I have felt heavenly intervention, times when someone held my hand and guided me through darkness, moments when I felt lost and was somehow led towards the right path by a higher power, the God soul.

---

*   Source: Rumi's works from 'Deewan-e-Shams Tabrezi' (original: Urdu, translation in Hindi, English)
    https://sufinama.org/persian-sufi-poetry/aan-ruuh-raa-ki-ishq-e-haqiiqii-shiaar-niist-rumi-persian-sufi-poetry-24?lang=hi.

Despite being a fully rational person and a man of science and reasoning, it is these supernatural yet real-life experiences that make one bow to the higher soul, realising its existence and blessings. It feels pre-destined—being introduced to Paramhans Dayalji and Shri Anandpur or the thought in my mind or the desire in recent years to understand the various 'why and how' questions in life and deepen the understanding of my spiritual side.

Turning to Philosophy

In recent years, I have found myself drawn to questions about life: why are we here? What is the purpose of life? How does one attain it? As a starting point, I tried to understand what philosophers throughout history have thought about these topics rather than reinventing the wheel. So I studied the foundations of various philosophical schools of thought from different parts of the world.

Though life has existed for millions of years, philosophy is less than 4,000 years old. The Indian Vedas are the oldest texts, dating back to 1400–1500 BCE.

I attempted to explore the history of philosophy across both the Western and Eastern worlds, from Thales, the first philosopher of the Western world from the sixth century BCE, to Greek, American and European thought. I inferred that Western philosophies tend to be outward-looking, focusing on the nature of existence, the world, life and non-life.

In contrast, Eastern philosophies—such as Japanese Zen, Chinese Taoism and the nine Indian philosophies (six Vedic: Samkhya, Yoga, Nyaya, Vaisheshika, Mimamsa, Vedanta; and three non-Vedic: Buddhism, Jainism, Charvak)—are more inward-looking, focusing on our existence, the purpose of life and conduct.

To my surprise, after more than twenty-five years of association with the Advaita Vedanta philosophical school of thought through Shri Anandpur, I have come to realise that Advaita Vedanta is one of the few philosophies of the world, besides Buddhism, that makes logical sense to even those not formally associated with it—and one that has been affirmed by science too.

Einstein's famous equation $E = mc^2$ expresses that energy (E), mass (m), and the speed of light (c) are related—meaning everything in the world, including all matter and humans, is a form of energy. This is consistent with Advaita Vedanta's teaching of non-dualism: that everything and everyone in the world is part of one Brahma element.

This whole journey sometimes makes sense only when looking backwards, as if there has been a plan for us all along.

Picking Up the Powerful Habit of Reading

I remember, as a fifth- or sixth-grade student, all I could think about at school was playing games and having fun with my friends, besides the curriculum coursework and lectures. I would sometimes notice a girl in class, Arushie Mangla, sitting alone at her desk, reading a book and smiling as if she was experiencing a whole different world inside that paperback.

Curiosity got the better of me one day, and I asked her about it. To my surprise, she offered me one of the novels she was reading, from *The Famous Five* series by Enid Blyton, based on the lives and adventures of a group of friends and their dog. Reading that book was like experiencing a different part of the world altogether, even while sitting nearly 7,000 miles away from the novel's actual setting.

From *The Famous Five* to the *Goosebumps* series and the Agatha Christies of the world, I began picking up pace in reading. By the time I reached the eighth or ninth grade, when I started reading J.K. Rowling's *Harry Potter* series, I was so addicted to reading that I would buy the latest edition on the day of its release. After school, around 2 p.m., I would read straight for eight to ten hours, finishing the 500+ page book cover to cover in a single night.

The next day at school, I would discuss the book with Arushie and other enthusiastic followers of the series who also finished it on launch day. Soon after, I encountered English literature, including Shakespeare and many others. Through this process, I inducted the powerful habit of reading into my daily life and eventually transferred this skill to other aspects of my life.

I have read for hours studying at school, during undergraduate and business school years, at work over the years and now when I spend most of my time reading. Whether it's work-related investor presentations, annual reports, quarterly results of companies, sector and industry reports or various other readings, these occupy most of my day. Sporadically, between this 'reading time', some time is spent with colleagues or externals such as management teams of businesses we are invested in or are evaluating or with some business promoters, or in self-learning, upskilling and exploring other interests.

The inference: reading is the not-so-hidden gem for wealth creation, financial independence and learning, and is arguably one of the best habits someone can inculcate, besides striving to live a healthy, prosperous and hopefully long life.

Little did I know back then that this skill would become one of my greatest strengths and a core competency in my field of work. Perhaps it is one of the best traits for any profession.

The Role of the Founders of Vidyamandir Classes

As mentioned earlier as well, during my high school years, when I began preparing for the IIT entrance examination, I enrolled in Vidyamandir Classes, run by three brothers, all IITians.

The learning curve was exponential, but what has stayed with me is the self-starter, problem-solving mindset and attitude they helped inculcate in me during those formative years. No matter how difficult a problem is, you apply yourself, try repeatedly and figure out a way to crack it, however long it takes—that was the philosophy we were taught. Once you are able to do that successfully, the self-reinforcing confidence it builds in your abilities is enormous. This problem-solving, self-starter mindset becomes ingrained in your system, shaping who you are as a person.

These learnings have helped me accomplish whatever I have set out to do, be it starting my own venture, persevering without giving up or finding solutions at work and in other aspects of life in general.

We used to call it the 'BCCR' mindset: be calm, cool and relaxed. These subtle inputs stay with us and are reinforced later in life when one realises the value of a clear, calm mind and the massive impact it can have when it becomes almost part of our DNA, consistently guiding the way we conduct ourselves.

It's like being Cristiano Ronaldo in a world where Messi is praised and worshipped. You may not be the best or most gifted person at the start, but by inculcating time-tested habits that compound over time, making you incrementally better at everything you do each day and eventually become one of the best, just like Cristiano did.

My Friend from IIT: Raghu

I met Raghu during the early days of my first year of undergraduate studies at IIT. The one person who has remained constant, the longest-lasting relationship in my life outside my spiritual relationship with Paramhans Dayalji and my family, is Raghu. Granted, he is family too by now, but you get the point.

True to his nature as a straight shooter, he has been my go-to person: as a friend, trusted advisor and sounding board for anything I wished to discuss. Most importantly, he has shown me the hard truths and facts whenever I have been delusional, helping me improve as a person throughout. Obviously, alongside this, are the softer aspects of our friendship and brotherly love, sharing all the different life experiences and time spent together over the years.

It is a handful of friends like these that we all need in life. Not the twenty so-called friends who are actually almost acquaintances we socialise with, who wish us on birthdays or party with us, but those few who stand by us regardless of how often they are physically present with us. They might even be in different parts of the world and meet rarely. They are the ones who show us reality whenever we speak, who would take a bullet for us and be by our side no matter what.

Ryan Boyle in My Professional Life

There are very few people at work who genuinely mean well for you, who are good at heart and one in a million who would go out of their way to help you learn, grow and evolve. Ryan Boyle, managing director at Goldman Sachs FIG EMEA Investment Banking in London, has been the Harvey (from the American TV series *Suits*) to my Mike.

He is practically a machine—disciplined, a lifelong learner and hardworking to the core. He taught me financial modelling on Excel at 3 a.m. during our time at Goldman, would take me along to meetings with CXOs of Fortune 500 companies when I was 'just' an analyst—the junior-most guy doing his job as required—even when he was not obliged to bring me along to such business meetings.

Junior people are like hands in such a setup, and the higher you rise through the ranks, the more your brain, business development and softer capabilities are leveraged. I could sense the borderline jealous looks on the faces of other bankers when they saw the output of our work or saw a junior analyst running a deal with a vice president (he was a VP when I was an analyst), with us as a team executing multi-billion-dollar deals end to end.

We were the dream team. Whether it was sheer luck or the plan of a higher power, I was in the right place at the right time, working with and learning from the best in the industry—and that has made all the difference in my work life.

The work ethic, dedication and mindset, the desire to be the best at what one does, refusing to do anything half-heartedly, and instead putting in the best effort without worrying about the immediate results have been invaluable lessons.

My Partner for Making Me Kinder, Compassionate and a Better Man

We've spoken about the pivotal impact my partner has had on my life and in shaping me into a better person. I believe any relationship is genuine and enduring when there is a true sense of companionship and comfort. There's this popular way of thinking that says that in a relationship, usually one person is a 'settler' and the other is a 'reacher'. It's rare when both people feel that they are the reacher in the relationship and are lucky to be with their partner who might have supposedly *settled* for them. If both feel this way, there is balance in the relationship. I am grateful for this feeling of pure admiration, sense of companionship and mutual respect besides love in our relationship.

It's when the other person makes you a better person, and you cannot imagine being who you are, how you are or where you are in life without their support. I truly understood and appreciated the concept of a soulmate after I met her.

And the Blessings of My Parents to Top It All

The power of parents' blessings is the true 'Bimtek' of my life. For their love, guidance, unconditional support and the fact that they never push or pressure any of their three children with expectations or desires, or expect us to live out their dreams rather than chart our own paths—these may seem basic when stated out loud, but it is a rarity, especially in India and with Indian parents.

Most of us do not appreciate the value of our elders' presence and advice while they are still around. It is only much later in life, through experience or reflection, that we realise how their presence and guidance serve as a steadfast North Star.

Almost my entire life, outside my professional circle, I have been introduced by my father's name—more as 'Chawla ji's beta' (son) and then 'Mohit Chawla'. It is the reputation of 'Chawla ji' that precedes me. It's these big shoes to fill: striving to make a name for myself while appreciating the privileges and reputation that come with that legacy.

Solo Travels

Solo travel has been an extension of what I learnt at Vidyamandir Classes during my formative years: being independent, a self-starter and having a problem-solving mindset.

Solo travelling can be a healing, therapeutic exercise. The time alone not only clears the mind but also cultivates the ability to independently manage everything, while absorbing and appreciating everything around in solitude. The quality of interactions with people, the time spent and the experience of exploring different cities, countries and cultures is deeply enlightening.

Personally, over the years I have embarked on multiple solo trips across India and internationally, with a twofold purpose. First, it is to absorb the surroundings and not be a tourist—to be more aware, open and appreciative of everything around me. The second reason is to engage in what I am supposedly good at—sitting and reading most days, often in nature, whether in the mountains, by the sea or a river or anywhere I am, immersed in peace, quiet and calm, to just absorb the surroundings and engage in deep work.

As much as I love socialising and spending time with my people, or those who matter most in my life, I consciously make it a point to take a solo trip every two years, whether in India or abroad. This is probably the equivalent of camping or fishing trips in the Western world, which people undertake every once in a while, alone or with family.

It is the exercise of being alone, planning and managing everything on one's own that sets things right for everyone in life.

Meditation and Enjoying My Own Company

Just like solo travelling, meditation has been a life hack that has stayed with me and deepened since my early teenage years because of my association with Shri Anandpur. It keeps me calm, centred and sane.

I appreciated how meditation improved my concentration and focus during my teenage years when I would meditate in the *amrit vela* (as the 3–5 a.m. time window is called), waking at 4 a.m. to meditate for half an hour and then study for three hours before school. It's difficult to describe how, after meditating, a three-hour morning study session felt far more productive and concentrated than double that time during regular day hours filled with distractions.

I am a self-proclaimed boring person. I prefer to keep my personal life private, am not very active on social media and keep my phone on do-not-disturb mode while working. I value being fully present in every activity I engage in, doing everything with all my head and heart and then moving on to the next task. Even simple acts, like brushing my teeth, become mindful exercises when you pay attention to the molars, premolars and canines. It's about awareness: being fully absorbed in the process of whatever we are doing, without distraction or dividing attention.

Some people use music to sharpen concentration and tune out noise; I have tried that and still do occasionally. However, clarity of thought gained through meditation and time alone probably tops my personal list for focus.

Shah Rukh Khan, Bollywood's king with over a billion followers worldwide, practises this. In an interview snippet, he describes spending a few hours alone each day, having a think, reflecting and clearing his head. That won my respect—not that he was seeking it—but because I had previously seen him only in mushy romantic comedies and exaggerated, larger-than-life films, which I didn't appreciate growing up. I'm glad to have been proved wrong about him.

Charpak, Eiffel Scholarship: HEC Paris, France and Cryptocurrencies

I was introduced to the world of cryptocurrency back in 2013, when Bitcoin wasn't as 'cool' as it is now and was not being compared to the tulip mania of the seventeenth century. Back then, it was simply a new concept of money: a peer-to-peer, decentralised medium of exchange, not yet necessarily viewed as digital gold.

My friend Akshay Datar, whom I met during undergraduate studies at IIT and later at HEC Paris, was an early rider of the crypto wave and introduced me to the idea. Initially, I wasn't particularly impressed by the concept of digital currency or a decentralised system without banks as intermediaries. I nearly dismissed it as a fad that was draining a friend's resources, both financially and time-wise. Regardless, live and let live is what I chose to make of it then.

As much as we all like to complain about the perceived sluggishness, the slow administrative process and fussiness of the French, I was pleasantly surprised by the generosity shown to bright young people like us, particularly students. Education in France—as in much of the developed world—is heavily subsidised, if not fully funded. During my time in Paris, a few of us were awarded the Charpak/Eiffel Scholarship by the French government for academic excellence at French institutions. This scholarship paid over 1,000 euros a month, a generous sum even after accounting for purchasing power parity.

Besides this, the CAF (Caisse des Allocations Familiales) provided students with financial support for accommodation, subsidising living expenses further. In my case this was an additional 300–500 euros a month. Altogether, a handsome sum of around 1,500 euros landed in my bank account every month, enabling me to live and experience French life, culture and cities and obviously study!

One fine day, while I was working on my entrepreneurial venture ideation at HEC Paris' entrepreneurship lab, Akshay was around studying and suggested that instead of spending the full 1,500 euros every month on what felt like a lavish student life, I should set aside that amount one month and invest it in cryptocurrencies.

Usually, I am not someone to act on second-hand information, but by dumb luck, this is one rare instance where I did. To be fair, I didn't necessarily act on second-hand information but more like I did not do full due diligence on the use cases or the potential utility value of cryptocurrencies back then. I barely spent a few hours on research—I read the Bitcoin white paper by Satoshi Nakamoto, Reddit discussions on cryptocurrencies and the general public consensus on their medium-term potential. Little did I appreciate back then the concept—that our head follows where our money is, or the principle of corporate finance that I was about to study a semester later, wherein management's interests should align with those of shareholders.

I realised that investing in cryptocurrencies actually sparked my interest in understanding the underlying blockchain technology and the diverse use cases of various digital currencies. Three months later, after detailed research, I invested more, this time in a basket of cryptocurrencies that I believed had solid use cases and the potential to change the world or at least some worldly ways.

As luck would have it, I have weathered various 'crypto winters' over the years, witnessing cryptocurrencies explode 100 to 1,000 times in value and then correct by 60–70 per cent every few years. Despite the volatility, the modest sums invested initially and incremental investments over time have grown into a substantial amount that alone could justify the title of this book!

This sum has now been duly set aside to fund the college education of my two nephews, and possibly the rest as a gift to them to try their hand at learning to invest later in life.

The lesson is not about random money-making or humblebragging but about being nimble and open to ideas: to diligence carefully, say no to most things and say yes only to those that genuinely make sense. Keep our pencils sharpened, and pounce on the few opportunities that do (make sense!).

Food/Cooking: Starting Something and Finishing It

Over time, I have come to believe that we inevitably cross paths with people we are meant to, those with whom we have some unsettled scores, whether to give or receive. Maybe it is karmic. Pranav Goyal is one such person in my life. A genuine, kind-hearted individual, he has taught me various life skills. Pranav and I shared an apartment for a few months when I was at HEC Paris.

The kind person that he is, he would cook Indian vegetarian meals for both of us. It was almost like experiencing motherly love through chapatis, sabzi, daal, rice and salad—essentially a full-course Indian meal 7,000 miles away from home. Why? No particular reason—just a kind, genuine person with no ulterior motive, who loved to cook and would do so for himself and for me.

Sometimes, we fail to appreciate these little things in life, the small contributions of those around us that seem obvious and trivial at the time, but cumulatively bring peace and comfort and allow us to focus on what truly matters and where we want to invest our energy.

Pranav taught me how to cook—making Indian bread, North Indian dishes like rajma chawal, daal, chole, mixed vegetable sabzi, kadhi chawal and many others, along with the basics of chopping vegetables and preparing the tadka (tempering) essential to these delicacies. He indirectly introduced me to the therapeutic nature of cooking, which led to my habit of cooking when I feel low or stuck in life. The simple exercise of cooking two-minute noodles, Nestle's Maggi, symbolising the mindset of not giving up: starting, doing and finishing. A lifelong lesson probably woven into my DNA by now!

I sometimes joke that Pranav was my brief experience of the borderline suppressed, oppressed homemaker wife from nineteenth-century India, who would care for her husband and family. In all fairness, looking back, Pranav is one of those rare people who, despite a limited time together, had a meaningful impact on me.

Writing on the Wall: The HEC e-lab

Most of us are either left-brained or right-brained. Very few of us are reasonably skilled across both or somewhere in between. That's just pure neuroscience—and by extension, pure luck—if someone happens to be such a person.

Early on, during high school, I realised I was good with numbers and maths, and therefore physics too. But studying engineering and architecture at IIT made me appreciate the creative side as well, something I hadn't recognised until then.

Many people opine that creative individuals sometimes lack business acumen, financial sense or the ability to switch between numeric logic and creative expression, but this doesn't necessarily have to be true.

There's a widely appreciated rule in architecture: *form follows function*—meaning the function of a building or spatial design is primary, and the design form must serve that function, not the other way around. Sometimes, architects design structures on a desktop in the artistic sense that are aesthetically pleasing but are rejected by structural engineers as functionally unviable.

Similarly, in business, the adage *cash is king* underscores that financial sense trumps everything. Some businesses might not make logical sense to outsiders but are financially viable, cash-chugging, profit-generating machines.

Having run a start-up as a twenty-something immediately after IIT and without a formal business degree, I realised that acquiring management knowledge and financial sense would be invaluable, especially early in my career. Thus, my time at HEC Paris epitomised the interplay of the left and right brain: crunching numbers and studying finance while working top-down on building an entrepreneurial venture.

I fondly recall spending days and nights in the entrepreneurship lab ('e-lab') at HEC Paris, practically living there—attending lectures, then spending the rest of the day eating, working and sometimes sleeping in the e-lab. It was pure hustle and flow of creative juices through and through. It was probably one of the times in my life where I could see the impact of the left and right brain combined to create magic; I felt like I was living through the best of times, the 'purple patch' of my life.

We would sit in the e-lab, scribbling on the wall: our big-picture plans, ideas and vision, and then zeroing down on the operational semantics. It's one of those times in life when work feels magical and true to heart to the extent that you think about it in your sleep, wake up with new ideas, rarely feel tired or drained, but instead feel the nervous excitement of creating something new—a 'high' like no other. It's like a batsman hitting the ball right out of the middle of the bat in cricket: the body, timing and game sense all align, and everything seems like a part of the golden run. It's well said that one should enjoy such moments while they last, for times change. There are days when we struggle to make any progress and each day feels like a push, but there also come periods like these when everything one touches turns to gold.

These experiences and learnings have stayed with me, as have the people who had a pivotal impact in defining the trajectory and path in my life. Humility is a virtue; expressing gratitude when due is the cherry on top.

Part III

Broader Learnings and Purpose of Life

13

Other Softer Aspects in Life

Benjamin Graham, Buffett's mentor and author of *The Intelligent Investor*, retired at sixty after achieving successful 20 per cent annual returns over his investment career. He spent the remaining twenty years of his life alternating between his homes in California and the south of France, writing, reading and savouring, in his own words, 'the world of the mind, from things of beauty and culture in literature and in art'. In his final years, when a journalist asked why he had quit investing in financial markets, Graham smiled warmly and replied, 'Why should I try to get any richer?' That, to me, is true wisdom!

Setting out on the conventional path to financial freedom and then reprioritising to experience the softer, more meaningful things in life the 'Graham way' is a sensible approach. To my mind, balancing life with equanimity, consistent with the mindset taught in the Bhagavad Gita of balance and equanimity in life makes the most sense.

While the 'Graham way' of experiencing and living and thereafter giving back later in life is admirable, my colleagues at Bimtek and I resonate more with and strive to live by the idea of doing things that have a meaningful impact during our lifetime, that we are able to make time for and, importantly, during our best years.

Bigger Purpose in Life

To my mind, every phase of life is dominated by certain activities:

- Phase 1: As a kid, playing.
- Phase 2: As a teenager, studying.
- Phase 3: Mid-twenties to mid-thirties, study and work, overlapping with familial duties and obligations.
- Phase 4: Mid-thirties to early fifties: excelling at work or craft alongside familial duties.
- Phase 5: Thereafter—based on the individual's journey and priorities—whether focusing on work, spending more time on personal life or working for a bigger cause, such as dedicating oneself to philanthropy or making a broader impact.

In my case, I have tried to balance these aspects starting from the latter half of the Phase 2 (above) and throughout Phase 3, aiming to live in an equanimous state in the second half of life, rather than compartmentalising activities strictly across different age and career phases.

This approach has reduced the stress of prioritising one area over others and allowed me to focus more on enjoying and absorbing the overall process of everything at hand, whether spending time with loved ones, working or creating wider impact.

Thinking About Our Existence/Purpose of Life?

As much as I am a man of science, my spiritual side has grown leaps and bounds over the past decade or two. One of the biggest reasons for this has been an inherent curiosity in knowing about us humans. Whether reading about our history or evolution, the fundamental question at the back of my mind has been about our existence: the human form, the various life forms around us and the purpose of the living being. More specifically, the purpose of human life keeps me intrigued.

I would be lying if I said I have it all figured out, but I continue to tread the path of enlightenment and spiritual awakening through meditation and following a spiritual guru, moving forward under their guidance.

It is said a coach or guru not only imparts knowledge but also guides us along the path we choose to follow. Finding answers to our existence has been a central quest in my thought process. In this regard, my spiritual learnings while following my guru, Shri Paramhans Dayalji, have been immense: in guiding me towards understanding the purpose of human life and its significance relative to other life forms, that is the estimated 8.4 million recognised species.

I believe this journey to enlightenment sometimes allows us to rise above the trivial day-to-day struggles and appreciate why we have been born—to fulfil both personal life goals and the broader purpose of the human form. It reveals how small we are as individuals in the larger scheme of life, yet how significant an impact we can make by doing our part. The realisation of the self can centre us during the trickiest situations, setting us apart from others and shaping our outlook and, thus, results in life.

It is that sense of detachment paired with composure in our thought processes that enables the highest and best performances in the most challenging times. As it is rightly said, identifying a problem or question is the first step towards solving it. The same holds for identifying and addressing the purpose of our lives. The path we choose to find our answers is subjective, whether through spirituality, self-realisation, enlightenment, karma or other routes. For instance, the concept of Islam regarding the purpose of life is that the kernel of true manhood is the ability to abandon sensual indulgence, i.e., not falling prey to the power of the senses. As Rumi writes, 'A saying of Muhammad is "Human awareness is my secret and I am its secret. The inner knowledge of spirit-essence is the secret within the secret. I have placed this knowing within the heart of my true servant, and no one can know his state but me. The knowing of essence is love's secret."'

This teaching broadly aligns with beliefs held in Hinduism as well.

Effective Altruism

I have aligned myself with and believe strongly in the philosophy of:

Being good, doing good. Always.

To that end, *effective altruism* is essentially about using our time and resources to help those around us to the best of our abilities. This is to be taken with a pinch of salt, as I was introduced to the concept during my time in Silicon Valley, a place where urban poverty coexists alongside entrepreneurs hustling in a highly stressful, sometimes toxic environment, and where the ultra-rich preach *effective altruism*.

The irony, if not sarcasm, is hard to miss. We encounter diverse people, ideas and philosophies every day, but clarity of thought enables us to differentiate good from bad and, crucially, not lose sight or focus and avoid being unduly influenced by inconsistent or unideal opinions.

Personally, I refer to this as the 'garbage-in, garbage-out' principle in the list of my mental models: wherein one listens to and absorbs everything around us but consciously reflects on it to screen out the noise from our system and prevent it from affecting our decision-making and thought processes.

To my mind, the simple way to understand effective altruism is that it involves using our ikigai—what we are good at and enjoy (commercially viable skills), combined with what society and the broader ecosystem truly need—and applying it in our daily lives to create positive impact in the lives of others.

Life Goals and Directional Sense

In pursuing these broader aspirations, I have never been a 'goals-driven' person in the conventional sense, never chasing one or more specific targets. Instead, I align with a directional sense of where I want to be and what I aspire to achieve, progressing one small step at a time in the right direction.

For example, I have identified three *focal points* or broad buckets of value creation:

a) Personal learning and development (including spiritual growth)
b) Family and friends
c) The nation and the broader ecosystem.

These broad buckets help me filter out noise and avoid wasting energy on endeavours that do not align or resonate with these core areas.

Alongside this, I hold a deep belief that no matter what I am doing or how I am feeling, consistency, discipline, patience and the blessings of my parents and a higher power will gradually bring me closer to what I set out to do. Over time, things normalise in the medium to long term, regardless of how challenging the circumstances may be.

Sticking to one's roots and keeping the *dhyaan*—mindfulness or focus—of the higher power at heart has guided me to the right place at the right time, the path of growth. This journey may be slow at times and accelerated at others, but it remains steady nonetheless.

Planning and Execution Toolkit: Long-Range Strategy, Next-Twelve-Month Plan, Weekly Progress and Daily Checklists

Ray Dalio, in his celebrated book *Principles of Life and Work*, outlines a five-step process for achieving goals in life:

1. Define your goals.
2. Identify the problems standing in the way of those goals.
3. Find the root causes of those problems.
4. Design or strategise ways to fix or work around these problems and root causes.
5. Work consistently to accomplish what you set out to do.

This iterative, feedback-loop process is consistent with the simple process of working from the ideation phase to devising a plan to execute the idea, and thereafter working on it with consistency, discipline and patience—something discussed earlier in Chapter 4. Sticking to the long-term directional objectives has served me well over the past few decades.

When it comes to day-to-day time management and resource allocation, my approach involves weekly planning and daily execution on an ongoing basis in the short term, while keeping directional check posts as medium-term milestones across quarters or the next twelve months and long-term strategic plans in mind. This set-up reinforces the concept of *pause and re-access* discussed earlier, enabling course correction if we feel stuck or are making minimal progress. It's akin to the 'think global, act local' mindset, which involves maintaining the big picture while taking focused action, or the 'zoom-in, zoom-out' approach.

Personally, I have further simplified these principles into broad buckets:

- Eating healthy and sleeping well, taking care of and respecting the body
- Setting aside regular time for meditation, spirituality and gratitude
- Ensuring ample time for work, personal learning and development
- Contributing to the ecosystem, such as mentoring colleagues or offering pro bono time without a personal agenda
- Having leisurely and quality time with family, friends and those who matter

I cannot recall ever meeting someone successful who doesn't read, nor someone without a plan in place or rules, checklists and frameworks guiding their path, be it simply planning our day or week or a broader personal plan. We call it being 'institutionalised' to a machine-like structure at large corporations where implementing broader strategies comes down to establishing structured processes and checklists to drive consistency and comfort in execution. Even an airplane pilot uses a checklist. I think you get the point: the simple act of creating rules, checklists or mental models is one of the easiest and most effective strategies to guide our endeavours on an ongoing basis.

Rising Above Ourselves

The genesis of my various learnings, whether professional, personal or otherwise, have been humbling, to say the least. The constant endeavour is to learn, grow and evolve, ultimately coming to the realisation that we are but a small part of a larger ecosystem and that, thus, it would be ideal to leverage our skillset to focus on a bigger purpose in life.

Finding our own passion is one challenge; being able to execute and achieve it is another. Taking care of our loved ones is one responsibility, but combining all our capabilities to create value for those around us and the broader ecosystem is yet another.

Some of us have this opportunity and are among the few fortunate ones to be born with privileges, having luck frequently on our side and access to the right resources, capabilities, networks and capital. Therefore, I believe it is a fiduciary duty for those of us so privileged to channel our time and resources meaningfully, to create impact beyond personal gains. It is not merely about making money or creating value for ourselves, but about delivering for the broader ecosystem—to rise above ourselves.

14

Principles of Life

Thus, for the first time since his creation, man will be faced with his real, his permanent problem—how to use his freedom from pressing economic cares, how to occupy the leisure, which science and compound interest will have won for him, to live wisely and agreeably and well.

—John Maynard Keynes

KEYNESIAN ECONOMICS HAS EARNED ADMIRATION FROM countries, leaders, economists and the investment world for John Maynard Keynes. Yet, to my mind, some of his life lessons transcend economics. His reflections question the modern man's purpose and the use of his time. Reading these has given me additional direction and purpose in life.

'Principles are fundamental truths that serve as the foundations for behavior that gets you what you want out of life. They can be applied again and again in similar situations to help you achieve your goals.' Ray Dalio, one of the most celebrated investors of modern times, has generously shared his principles of life through a book and a series of blogs.

Inspired by Dalio's life and *Principles*, alongside learnings from great minds across industries and scholars who have studied the most successful people of their times, I have attempted to compile a synopsis of 'directional guidance' principles from various fields that have helped me be a 'Jack of most trades, not master of one' and to lead a more fulfilling, purposeful life.

These reference learnings in this chapter are structured into four buckets:

a) Spiritual learnings
b) Personal learnings
c) Professional learnings
d) Learnings based on precedents of some of the best in the world

This effort is about sharing knowledge and recognising that life is not a zero-sum game—one person's win isn't another's loss. It is a broader journey where we learn from those far older and wiser, as well as from younger minds with fresh ideas and experiences.

It is a reminder to remain humble, appreciating and absorbing the wisdom of those who came before us. Currently, there are 8 billion people living in the world, but multiple times of that number who are collectively dead and passed on their experiences. This is about cultivating a growth mindset, about becoming a better person each day: by reading and learning from the experiences of others and sharing that wisdom for the benefit of all.

Spiritual Learnings: Paramhans Dayalji's Grace

It is believed that the purpose of human life is the unification of our soul with the higher soul—*aatma ka parmatma se milan*—or *aatamgyan* (self-realisation), which is the source of enlightenment. By extension, one can fulfil life's purpose by keeping God in our hearts while fulfilling our human duties, whether familial or worldly, without extreme attachment.

It is also believed that worldly desires cannot co-exist with the pure desire to attain this purpose, in our hearts. However, one may fulfil all worldly desires, should one remain focused on the core purpose. Paramhans Dayalji often said in his *pravachans* (teachings):

Tum prabhu ke naam par toh wo tumhare kaam par
Tum apne kaam par toh prabhu apne dhaam par
(If you keep God in your heart, he will take care of everything you seek or desire.)

He emphasised five daily principles for our self-realisation and fulfilling the purpose of human life: *Shri Aarti Pooja, Seva, Simran, Satsang aur Dhyaan* (praying, giving back, meditation, spiritual learning/discussion, and mindful appreciation of oneness with the God soul—non-dualism and equanimity in conduct). By practising meditation and following these five principles, I have been able to maintain a centred mind, prioritise the things and people that matter, focus on what I wish to accomplish and conduct myself to lead a fulfilling and equanimous life.

My love for God and desire to embrace Paramhans Dayalji's lessons have instilled discipline and consistency in me from an early age. The compound effect of this discipline, combined with the equanimity and focus meditation provides, has impacted not just my spiritual journey but also catalysed my personal and professional endeavours. This is something I would encourage readers to explore as well.

Bhagavad Gita: Learnings

I have read the Bhagavad Gita several times. Among the various versions and translations available, I am particularly drawn to *The Bhagavad Gita: As It Is* by Swami Prabhupada.

I have also explored spiritual and religious literature across traditions such as Hinduism, Buddhism, Jainism, Taoism and Zen. Remarkably, the core teachings seem consistent across most of these philosophies.

For context, the Bhagavad Gita was delivered by Shri Krishna to Arjun during the battle of Mahabharata and represents the essence of all Vedic literature. Its origins trace back from Lord Shri Krishna to Lord Surya, then to Manu and onward through the ages.

The Bhagavad Gita is said to serve the purpose of delivering mankind from the entanglements of material existence. It is an inquiry into human existence and purpose.

The image here from the Bhagavad Gita indicates how, when one follows worldly desires, one is going down a path of pain and deterrence while detachment from worldly desires as well as keeping higher soul at heart is the path to enlightenment, liberation and unification of the soul with a higher power (God soul).

Sat-Chit-Anand: (Sachidanand): Being, Knowledge, Bliss

The Bhagavad Gita encompasses the comprehension of five basic truths: Ishvar (God), Jeev (the living entity), Prakriti (nature), eternal time and karma (activity). Among these, God, living entities, material nature and time are eternal. Though the manifestation of Prakriti may be temporary, it is not false.

The Bhagavad Gita teaches that we must purify our materially contaminated consciousness. It does not advocate ceasing all activity; rather, it calls for the purification of our activities, through *bhakti* (devotional service). Desire for overlording and sense gratification are the greatest enemies of the conditioned soul, yet through the strength of consciousness, one can control the material senses, mind and intelligence.

One need not abruptly abandon work or human duties, but by gradually cultivating higher consciousness, it is possible to reach a transcendental state, remaining uninfluenced by material senses and the mind, through steady intelligence focused on one's pure identity.

Yoga and Meditation: Path to Self-realisation, Enlightenment

In simple terms, yoga means linking our consciousness with the absolute truth. Different practitioners name this linking process differently based on their chosen method.

When the focus of this process of linking is predominantly on fruitful activities, it is called *karma-yoga*—where a person knows life's goal but remains detached from the fruits of their actions. When the focus is on mental speculation to understand God, it is called *jnana-yoga*. When the practice is predominately a devotional relationship with the higher power (God soul), it is called *bhakti-yoga*. And when consciousness is fully absorbed in devotional service, it is called *buddhi-yoga* or *bhakti-yoga*.

Bhakti-yoga is considered the ultimate perfection of all yogas, rich in spiritual knowledge. Yoga essentially means *bhakti-yoga*, with other yogas serving as progressions leading towards it. The journey from *karma-yoga* at the beginning to *bhakti-yoga* at the end is a long path to self-realisation.

According to the Bhagavad Gita, the path to enlightenment can be broken into four stages:

1. Stage of knowledge
2. Stage of meditation
3. Stage of understanding the higher power (God soul)
4. Stage of the supreme personality of the higher soul— imbibing the personality traits of the higher soul in life. For example, the *Ramcharitmanas* describes the persona of Lord Ram.

Transcendental Qualities of an Enlightened Person

A person who is not envious, but a kind friend to all; who does not see themselves as a proprietor; who is free from false ego; who maintains equanimity in both happiness and distress; who is always satisfied, engaged in service to others with determination and whose mind and intelligence are in alignment—these are the qualities of an enlightened person.

In spiritual thought, there are three modes of the human mind, faith or material nature:

- Mode of ignorance: general lack of interest, laziness, obliviousness
- Mode of passion: attachment to worldly wealth and desires

- Mode of goodness: the path to enlightenment.

The role of a spiritual guru is to help one progress from laziness (ignorance) to passion, then to goodness and finally onto the path of enlightenment.

An enlightened soul is satisfied with all that life brings, avoids anger and the gratification of the senses and remains free from false ego and attachment to material things. This stage is self-realisation, wherein freedom from material conceptions grants deep peace, and such a person can rarely be agitated.

The bestselling book *The 7 Habits of Highly Effective People* by Stephen R. Covey draws inspiration from teachings including the Bhagavad Gita and Mormon Christian faith. This is another indication that these spiritual learnings are an essential aspect of material success.

Personal Learnings

Adam Smith: NOT Economics but Human Nature and Happiness

Adam Smith is renowned for his influence in economics, but his other seminal work, *The Theory of Moral Sentiments*, is often overlooked despite being a foundational insight into human nature and happiness.

In this work, Smith introduces the concept of the *iron law of me*, which highlights how we tend to think much more about ourselves than everyone else around while, in reality, others pay much less attention to us than we imagine. On this basis, imagining an impartial spectator to our actions, deeds and words makes us act morally, behave with more empathy and be a better person overall. Smith explores what makes us happy and gives life meaning—the pursuit of goodness and virtue. He argues that true happiness stems from contributing to the lives and successes of others, making the path of altruism both valuable and rewarding.

Being Loved and Being Lovely Is the Real Source of Happiness in Life

People desire not only to be loved but to be *loveable*—meaning worthy of being loved. It's not about money or fame, but about embodying qualities that make us deserving of love. Inherently, seeking wisdom and virtue is more fulfilling than pursuing material fame; this path naturally earns us love, respect and makes us genuinely good and lovely.

Simply put: *Be good, do good. Say little, do much.*

Mark Manson, in his book *The Subtle Art of Not Giving a F*ck,* succinctly expresses this idea:

> To be happy, we need something to solve. Happiness is therefore a form of action. It's an activity, not something that is passively bestowed upon us, not something that we magically discover in a top article in the newspaper.
>
> We don't find it waiting for us in a place, an idea, a job, or even a book. Happiness is a constant work-in-progress, because solving problems is a constant work-in-progress. The solutions to today's problems will lay the foundation for tomorrow's problems, and so on. True happiness occurs when we find the problems we enjoy having and solving.

Happiness, Health and Priorities in Life

'There is no path to happiness. Happiness is the path.'

—Buddha

The key to a good life lies not in caring about more, but in caring about less—specifically, caring only about what is true, immediate and important.

Ironically, the desire for more positive experiences is itself a negative experience. Conversely, accepting one's negative experiences is itself a positive experience. Learning to focus and prioritise thoughts effectively, choosing what truly matters based on refined personal values, is an exceptionally difficult task. It takes a lifetime of practice and discipline, with regular setbacks along the way, but it may be the most worthwhile struggle we can undertake. Essentially, it means not caring about minor things, caring deeply about the important things, decluttering our minds and simplifying thoughts so that unimportant things do not bother us!

Satisfaction

Satisfaction doesn't necessarily come from merely achieving goals or success but from struggling well through life's challenges. Since life naturally includes ups and downs, struggling well doesn't just make our ups better, it makes our downs less bad.

As poetic souls have said, *the journey is more important than the destination.*

Sometimes, people achieve success or peak early in life. In case they struggle to find something bigger and better in life to struggle for thereafter, they end up unhappier than before. Such is the irony of life.

Richer, Wiser and Happier

Essentially, we need to focus on simplifying life by following straightforward principles—such as aiming to be *directionally right* rather than striving for perfection or risking being outrageously wrong.

Other key drivers of well-being include maintaining brain health through exercise, meditation and good nutrition. Being decent and kind, treating others as we wish to be treated, while compounding goodwill by helping and uplifting others and giving back builds long-term incremental advantage.

A simple way for contentment, happiness and likely success lies in consciously choosing who we spend our time with and our relationships, while hedging against our own fallibility.

Values, Problems and the Quality of Our Lives

Our values determine the nature of our problems, and the nature of our problems determines the quality of our lives. To change how we perceive our problems, we must change what we value and how we measure failure and success.

Good values are reality-based, socially constructive and controllable, while bad values tend to be superstitious, socially destructive and beyond our immediate control.

Some ideal values include:

1. *Radical responsibility*: Taking ownership of everything in our life, regardless of who is at fault.
2. *Uncertainty*: Recognising our own ignorance and cultivating continuous doubt in our own beliefs.
3. *Failure*: Willingness to identify our flaws and mistakes to improve.
4. *Rejection*: The ability to say no and accept no, clearly defining boundaries for what we will and will not tolerate in life.

5. *Contemplation of mortality*: Reflecting on our own death is perhaps the only thing capable of helping us keep our values in proper perspective.
    As Warren Buffett famously advises:

'Write your obituary and figure out how to live up to it.'

The Self-Awareness Onion: Layers

Being self-aware is akin to recognising a problem so that we can identify its root cause and work to resolve it. Similarly, self-awareness plays a crucial role in personal growth.
    Self-awareness is often understood in layers:

* *First layer*: A basic recognition and understanding of one's emotions
* *Second layer*: The ability to ask why we feel certain emotions, identifying root causes to enable change or improvement
* *Third layer*: Examining our personal values—why we define success or failure as we do, how we choose to measure ourselves and by what standards we judge ourselves and others.

Perspective and the Bigger Picture: Elephant and the Ten Blind Men

To conclude personal learnings, a Buddhist fable comes to mind: ten blind men each encounter an elephant and describe it based on their experience of the elephant. Each ends up holding a different part of the elephant. One feels the trunk, another the tail, another the belly and so forth. Each perceives the elephant differently—as a snake or coil (from the trunk or tail), a big round surface (from the belly) or a solid pillar (from the legs)—yet none comprehends the might of the elephant.

This fable has been repeatedly referenced by the Upanishads and Jain and Islamic texts and many other philosophical traditions to illustrate the limitations of a single perspective. Looking at things through just one lens can distort reality. A broader, bigger-picture view requires considering multiple facets and perspectives to gain holistic understanding. This is why a multifaceted approach in life is essential.

Professional Learnings

Emotional Quotient: Why EQ Matters More Than IQ

American psychologist Daniel Goleman emphasises the importance of slowing down and conducting root cause analysis rather than reacting impulsively to words influenced by emotions like anger. This emotional awareness is crucial because even the smartest person can fall prey to emotional pitfalls. As such, it is rightly said that the long-term game is often won by emotional intelligence (EQ), not just IQ.

Making Logic One Tool in Life and NOT the Tool

Rory Sutherland, in his book *Alchemy*, builds on this idea by advocating for logic to be just one tool among many in life, not the sole guide. He encourages exploring non-logical or psychological approaches, questioning the status quo through simple 'why' questions where real breakthroughs often occur.

Sutherland opined that the need to appear scientific, and using purely logical methodology can prevent us from considering creative, magical solutions that might be cheaper, faster and more effective. While logic often wins arguments, it is not necessarily the best approach in all endeavours. Entrepreneurs like Steve Jobs, James Dyson, Elon Musk and Peter Thiel have acquired unprecedented wealth precisely because they break free from conventional logic and committee-driven decisions, sometimes appearing unconventional or 'bonkers'.

The trick to being an 'alchemist' lies in recognising when universal laws of logic do not apply, as human behaviour is inconsistent and not always governed by universal rational laws. For instance, although a utilitarian would expect consistent altruism, people vary greatly in whom they help or cooperate with.

Imagine you get into financial trouble and ask a rich friend for a loan of ₹10 lakh. But he patiently explains that you are a much less deserving case for support than an NGO supporting children's education in a village, to which he plans to donate the same amount. Your friend is behaving perfectly rationally. Unfortunately, he would no longer be your friend!

'A mind all logic is like a knife all blade. It makes the hand bleed that uses it.'

—Rabindranath Tagore

Or as wise people say, relying solely on rational arguments limits us to using only a portion of our full set of tools. Logic demands a direct, clear connection between reason and action, whereas psychological thinking allows for more nuanced, indirect pathways, acknowledging that human behaviour often operates beyond straightforward rationality. This broader perspective enables more creative, flexible and effective approaches to understanding and influencing outcomes.

Context Is Important

Why? In the book *Skin in the Game*, Nassim Nicholas Taleb presents a thought-provoking perspective on an individual's politics: a person's political alignment can vary by context—for example, libertarian at the federal level, republican at the state level, democrat in their town, socialist within their family and Marxist with their pet. Each role is shaped by specific needs and abilities.

This highlights the crucial role of *context* in shaping how people think, behave and act. Such variability challenges the viability of universal models, because rationalists must often ignore context to formulate universal laws.

Apparently, Niels Bohr once told Einstein he wasn't really thinking but merely being logical. Having a logical approach to problem-solving helps us believe we are on a path to solutions grounded in conventional reasoning. However, this approach can prevent us from exploring less logical, more imaginative solutions that break conventions or maybe sheer 'luck' leading to innovation.

Logical thinking may restrict counterintuitive approaches. To my mind, this resonates with Charlie Munger's advice: 'In life, always invert!'

This essentially means to look at things the other way around. Be it back-solving, reverse engineering or not necessarily being logic-bound.

An extension of this idea is the notion that *value lies in the mind and heart of the valuer*. Similar to *'beauty lies in the eyes of the beholder'*, human psychology can transform perception and create 'alchemy', turning something ordinary into something precious by altering how it is viewed. For instance, the worth of paperback books or fine art, jewellery and collectibles often depends on perception rather than intrinsic form.

Most successful businesses, like Google and Apple, have either figured out or been lucky to stumble upon this 'mental alchemy', creating premium products and services that command high value through shaping perception as much as through substance. Let that thought brew!

Letting Go of the Ego

As Ryan Holiday states in his book *Ego Is the Enemy*, ego is the enemy of what we want and what we have; it hinders mastery of a craft, creative insight, working well with others, building loyalty and support, longevity and the ability to sustain success. Ego repels opportunities and advantages. It's a magnet for enemies and mistakes. Zeroing down on obstacles and cracking on is the way.

We cycle through three mental states in life:

1. Aspire
2. Fail
3. Succeed

We aspire until we succeed, succeed until we fail or set new aspirations and after failure, we begin aspiring or succeeding again. The guiding principle is: Be humble in aspirations, resilient in failure and gracious in success.

As a wise man once said:

A man's best treasure is a thrifty tongue. Talk depletes us.

Humility and Appreciation

A famous story from thirteenth-century Persian poet Rumi's *Masnavi* illustrates a profound lesson in humility and appreciation of diverse skills.

A learned scholar crossing a river by boat asked the boatsman if he had studied. The boatsman humbly replied, 'No, sir.' The scholar arrogantly remarked that the boatsman had wasted his life by not acquiring knowledge. Moments later, a storm struck, and the boatsman asked the scholar if he knew how to swim. Bewildered, the scholar said no. The boatsman gently pointed out that the scholar, despite his education, had wasted his life by not learning a crucial skill to survive the situation and then jumped off the boat.

This story reminds us to appreciate the intricacies of different skillsets and fields, along with the humility that comes from recognising the limits of our own knowledge. Forming opinions based on limited experience can be futile. And thus, the importance of appreciating the knowledge and learning of people across diverse disciplines in life.

Being a Lifelong Learner and Student

To my mind, the power of being a student is not just that it is an extended period of instruction; it also places the ego and ambition in someone else's hands. Passion is *form over function*. Purpose is *function, function, function*.

The critical work we want to do requires deliberation and consideration. Not passion. Not naïveté. It requires dispassionate focus and action. Greatness comes from humble beginnings; it comes from grunt work. It means we are probably the least important person in the room—until we change that with results.

Our own path, whatever we aspire to, will in some ways be defined by the amount of nonsense we are willing to deal with. Getting angry, emotional, losing restraint—these are likely recipes for failure in the ring. Restraint is a difficult skill, but a critical one. We are all often tempted, sometimes even overcome. No one is perfect with it, but try we must!

Magic of Writing Things Down

I believe that writing is the purest form of thinking. One often comes across the saying that clarity of a concept emerges when it is explained to someone else in the simplest of terms that even a five-year-old could understand. Writing takes this one step further. Writing down what we wish to accomplish, are thinking about or are already working on, not only reinforces it in our mind but also clears it in a sense that it forces us to think, to organise our thoughts and to refine them further.

I can count numerous occasions where I have improved my work simply because, as a writer, it made me think deeper, explore directions I might not otherwise have considered and thus emerge stronger and clearer.

I may not be an expert, but writing requires the compression of an idea into its building blocks. When done poorly, it strips out insights; when done well, it retains the insights and removes the excess. It therefore demands both thinking and understanding, which is a primary reason why writing is so important.

In today's context, artificial intelligence and the ChatGPTs of the world may serve as tools for writing, just as every tool in human history has aided our advancement but has not taken over our writing, because we think.

The inherent advantage of the human mind is its ability to think, to innovate and not merely interpret data like artificial intelligence or a machine learning device would.

Half the Secret of Life: Obsession and a Long Attention Span

I'm not a polymath. I am a person who has been able to take moderate obsession and a long attention span and turn them into pretty good results. I believe a long attention span will help you a great deal if you're reasonably smart.

If you're obsessed with something, even intermittently, and you have a long attention span, keeping at the serious problems will likely lead you to stumble upon an answer. That's half the secret of life!

Why I Almost Worship Reason

Charlie Munger once famously said, 'I almost worship reason.' You could argue that Henry Singleton did as well and Warren Buffett certainly does too. The people I know who are good believe we have a duty to become as wise as we can be by constantly studying and thinking about things.

I have a living example in my life—my father, a self-made, self-educated man. I have watched him, and his life has worked out pretty well. He has not been making many mistakes.

Looking Inwards: Luxury Goods of Life

Putting Money in Its Place

The biggest luxury of being financially well, I've realised, is ensuring that money doesn't have an outsized influence on any of the major decisions we make and that it doesn't cause stress.

For example, has the price of flights or hotels for my specific travel date gone up since we first looked at them? Not ideal, but I would stick with the plan in case the airline or online travel agent's dynamic pricing doesn't bring it back near earlier prices by the time I ideally want to get the bookings done. The peace of mind that comes with having money in the bank, or in my case, my investment account, isn't a conventional luxury good, but it's one I treasure far more than I ever could an uber-expensive car, watch or bag.

As I've grown older and have had more funds at my disposal, a funny thing has happened. I'm much less inclined to want or need to show what I have than I was when I had far less. My 'luxury goods' today are much more in the category of things that make me feel good inside rather than look good on the outside.

And they're not 'things' at all. Over the years, many financially well-off people have shared variations of the same sentiment: their need for outward shows of success has been inversely correlated with their net worth.

Luxury Goods: Being Able to Help

One of my very favourite luxury goods has been the ability to extend financial help to people when they've needed it, especially to the less fortunate, without doing any PR around it.

For instance, I have never seen my father talk to people about the charity he does, or where and what he does in his philanthropic endeavours. I have seen it up close, and his philosophy is '*Ek haath se do toh doosre ko bhi pata na chale*' (Do whatever you can best, without drawing attention to it).

Being able to make an impact in someone's life when you do not necessarily have to, and the satisfaction of seeing that impact, is probably the best feeling. A luxury, a pure sense of happiness.

Most of Us Eventually or At Least a Couple of Times, Get Our Opportunity in Life

Everything takes time. It's about patience—keeping your sanity intact, your pencils sharpened and going at it with hard work, dedication and consistency. Hard work doesn't necessarily make us luckier; rather, putting in a lot of work positions us so that we see more opportunities and are prepared to pounce on them because we are ready.

Financial Independence and Making Money Work for Us

A lot of people talk about financial independence and retiring early, 'F.I.R.E' as they call it. Someone once told me that financial independence is when *interest-on-interest* can sustain our lifestyle.

In India, a bank fixed deposit can earn around 6 per cent in the current interest rate environment. Essentially, the interest on this 6 per cent is another 6 per cent, that is, 6 per cent of 6 per cent, or 0.0036 times the principal per year.

Depending on our annual living expenses, one can easily calculate the magic number by dividing the annual expenses by 0.0036. For example, for someone living in a Tier-1 metro city in India and spending ₹1 lakh per month, or ₹12 lakh per year on living, lifestyle and familial expenses, this calculation would give a figure of almost ₹30–35 crore INR.

Alternatively, investing in a mutual fund scheme that proxies India's growth over the long term would yield 10–12 per cent returns per year, making the interest-on-interest calculation roughly 10 per cent of 10 per cent, i.e., 1 per cent of the principal. The magic number here would be ₹12 lakh divided by 1 per cent, or essentially ₹12 crore or $1.5million for a lavish lifestyle.

There are others who follow the '*4 per cent rule*', which says once our lifestyle expenses fall under 4 per cent of our overall income per year, or our annual income is twenty-five times our annual expenses, one can be considered financially independent.

Thus, for living expenses ranging between ₹50,000 to ₹2 lakh per month, the magic number would range from ₹1.5–6 crore or $200,000–1 million. This is the genesis of the aspirational '*millionaire*' tag that most people pursue.

To my mind, financial independence means not having to think about money ever in life for anything, be it purchasing something one wishes to buy or travelling by whichever means, whether business-class airline travel and five-star hotel stays or economy travel and a basic two- to three-star motel at a riverside camp. The fundamental idea is not having to worry about or think of money as a constraint.

The Bhagavad Gita also notes that '*tyaag se pehle bhog zaruri hai*'. (One needs to experience things before giving up on them to appreciate the true sense of detachment).

I have been fortunate enough to reach that stage in life and state of mind where buying things to maintain a lifestyle or project a certain status in society—be it a house, a fancy car, wearing $300 Burberry shirts every day, $5,000 Rolex or Omega watches, Armani suits or any other material possession—no longer excites me, nor does seeking validation or judgement from others matter.

Why? Financial independence, the peace of mind at heart and the comfort it brings have made me detached and possibly rise above these aspects or behaviours in the literal sense of the words.

The suggestion for readers here is to start investing 'early', as it can be one of the best paths to financial independence, besides maintaining a modest lifestyle. 'Early' here means whenever one appreciates the idea of investing to grow net worth rather than just relying on the next salary slip to sustain life.

I started investing small in my late teenage years and more in my early twenties. I learnt that Warren Buffett made his first investment when he was eleven years old, and he says he was late. The point I am trying to make is, no time is too early, nor is it ever too late.

Not saving and investing is the only fallacy. Besides financial freedom, I used to look at freedom as the ability to do what I want when I want. If I make enough money, then I'm in control of my supposed 'destiny'.

My interactions and learnings from Jawad Mian, an investor and blogger, made me appreciate that this idea was flawed. Since very few people ever achieve financial independence, it cannot be the universal ideal. And what good is financial freedom if one is captive to negative thoughts and feelings?

The idea should be to achieve personal freedom, to liberate oneself from the burdens of past regrets, traumas or negative experiences that hinder personal growth and well-being; to be free from worries about the future regardless of financial status; to be unaffected by what others may think of us so that we can make conscious choices that align with our own values and aspirations. Personally, I choose to live a faith-centred life that is not afraid of death.

As Jawad rightly said,

True freedom is not the money kind. It comes from inner peace, contentment, and a sense of empowerment in the present moment.

Precedents: Standing on the Shoulders of Giants

Roger Federer: Transformation from the Angry Young Man to the Master

I remember growing up watching Roger Federer play tennis. I've been fortunate to see him rise through the ranks, from when he started acing greats such as Andre Agassi, Pete Sampras and Andy Roddick, to owning the grass courts and consistently being the world's best tennis player.

His classic matches against Rafael Nadal, Djokovic and Andy Murray—the top four of their era, along with him—and later when he almost gave the generation after him, including Tsitsipas, Stefanos and the likes, a run for the top spot, essentially showcased his longevity, consistency, discipline and depth of character.

Not sure if some of you remember, but the calm, cool, ever-so-centred and one of the greatest players of modern-day tennis, arguably the gentleman of the game, Federer was not the same when he started off. I remember seeing Federer as any other up-and-coming professional tennis player: flamboyant, full of energy, talented and aggressive, sometimes with borderline anger or frustration, when one would see him curse or slam rackets on the court during matches he was losing or not playing well.

Later, he evolved into arguably the greatest of all time (G.O.A.T.) and a man of conduct, honour, integrity and character. He's the epitome of good conduct both on and off the court, be it in his familial endeavours, spending time with and caring for his kids, wife and parents, or on the tennis court and outside with anyone and everyone.

Learning six different languages besides Swiss German to conduct interviews in other international languages after a long, tiring game; spending time with ball boys or young aspiring players, guiding them; and making time to socialise with people coming to meet and spend time with the legend—all demonstrate his character.

I had the fortune of meeting him once at a café in his hometown of Basel, Switzerland. Being the fanboy that I am, I was awestruck. The humble champion literally introduced himself by saying, 'Hi! I'm Roger.' Yes, the greatest player of all time introduced himself as if I didn't know of his existence or was possibly living under a rock all my life. Such is his humility. I ended up getting a couple of autographs from him, and due credit to his sense of humour, when he signed the fourth or fifth item, he asked, 'I hope you are not going to sell these?'

I remember writing about him in my personal journal almost a decade ago when my mind realised the genius of the man—his hard work, dedication, consistency, discipline and persistence—which led to this 'magic' of becoming the master of the game and a gem of a person both on and off the court. I have looked up to him as one of the inspirational anchors in my life, both for his journey and his character. Stories such as these are hiding in plain sight, which most of us acknowledge yet fail to fully appreciate the depth of. This is what we should aspire to do.

There are many similar examples of characters, sportspersons and people from different domains who have become the best in their respective fields and inspired millions. It is the depth of their character, and their consistency in learning, unlearning and doing the boring (not so sexy!) stuff each day that has produced the 'magic' for them. Be it Mahendra Singh Dhoni, Virat Kohli, Cristiano Ronaldo, Roger Federer, Michael Jordan, Warren Buffett—the list is endless!

Afterword

Fortunate are those who are able to make sense in the chaos around us.

THROUGHOUT THE VARIOUS CHAPTERS IN THIS BOOK, I HAVE tried to share my thoughts and life lessons that have directed me to what and where I am in my life and, more importantly, who I am as a person.

Some of these basic building blocks, if done right over a long period, lead to a compound effect in personal wealth, prosperity, well-being and peace—both in heart and mind—and around us in relationships, society and the ecosystem at large.

The story culminates with these principles of life that have served me well and likely shall for readers too. Broadly, these have been grouped under various headers across the three parts of the book:

1. ***Personal life***: Through my parents' ('Bimtek') value system, sanskaars and lessons—both good and bad, wins and defeats beautiful and not so—that have humbled me and given me pain, pleasure and, importantly, learnings. Each step as an opportunity to introspect, reflect and build on becoming a better person. Also included are spiritual learnings through my association with Shri Anandpur Trust and Paramhans Dayalji, as well as experiences with and insights about different religions, faiths and meditation at large, helping rise above our trivial day-to-day struggles to understand and appreciate the purpose of human life and general conduct. This appreciation has kept me centred, maintaining equanimity, calm and composure in the most challenging life situations.

2. ***Professional life***: Through working with and under the guidance of some of the best people across industries and geographies worldwide. It is about the idea of giving back, not just personally and socially, but also professionally. It is about investing in people and the broader ecosystem. And at the individual level, it means defining our vision, desires and dreams and sticking to the process of moving from the ideation phase to devising a plan to work on the idea and thereafter working on it with consistency, discipline and patience. Sticking to long-term directional objectives and keeping at it has worked out just fine for me over the past few decades. It's about keeping things simple and sticking to the plan each day, which works wonders over the long term.

4. ***Readings***: 'Standing on the shoulders of giants'—learning from some of the best, most successful people and their biggest mistakes—and boy, has that helped! Not only to say 'no' and avoid pitfalls but also to cut through the noise and focus on the low-hanging fruits in life. The primary understanding is

that life doesn't have to be difficult or made difficult by our choices; it can be made much simpler and more efficient if we keep our eyes and ears open to the wisdom from some of the best people who were gracious enough to share their experiences and learnings for all of us to absorb and apply.

How can we all be happier, wiser and hopefully richer? For happiness is like a butterfly—the more we chase it, the more it eludes us. The moment we focus on our tasks, it quietly comes and shrugs our shoulders like a cool breeze.

It is the trust in the process—that everything eventually normalises with effort—or the fact that worldly success and money somehow just follows.

And overall, living a healthy lifestyle with gratitude and principles that define our character is a tried and tested 'simple but not easy' route to peace of mind, clarity and a better life overall.

Such has been the aspiration behind writing this book.

Not to inspire, but to encourage. Not to guide, but to suggest.

To push some of you readers to find the best version of yourselves. To cut through the noise around us, find our true purpose—our personal ikigai—and make an impact in whatever we choose to do!

Bibliography

Ari Kiev, *Hedge Fund Masters: How Top Hedge Fund Traders Set Goals*, Overcome Barriers, and Achieve Peak Performance, Wiley, 2005.

Chanakya Neeti, *Penguin Random House*, 2020.

Coleman Barks, *Rumi: The Book of Love*, Poems of Ecstasy and Longing, HarperOne, 2005.

Daniel Goleman, *Emotional Intelligence: Why it can matter more than IQ*, Bantam Books, 1995.

Edward Morris, *Wall Streeters: The Creators and Corruptors of American Finance*, Columbia University Press, 2015.

Jalaluddin Rumi, *The Book of Love*, Coleman Barks, 2003.

John Gribbin, *Deep Simplicity: Bringing Order to Chaos and Complexity*, Random House, 2004.

John Kenneth Galbraith, *The Essential Galbraith*, Library of America, 2010.

Karim R. Lakhani and Marco Iansiti, *Competing in the Age of AI: Strategy and Leadership When Algorithms and Networks Run the World*, The Harvard Business Review Press, 2020.

Mark Manson, *The Subtle Art of Not Giving a F*ck: A Counterintuitive Approach to Living a Good Life*, HarperOne, 2016.

Maryam Mafi, *The Book of Rumi: 105 Stories and Fables That Illumine*, Delight, and Inform, Penguin Compass, 2021.

Pancham Padshahiji's New Granth, Shri Anandpur Satsang Ashram (Trust).

Pancham Padshahiji's Pravachan, Shri Anandpur Satsang Ashram (Trust).

Ray Dalio, *Principles: Life and Work*, Avid Reader Press/Simon & Schuster, 2017.

Robert B. Cialdini, *Influence: The Psychology of Persuasion*, Harper Business, 2006.

Roger Fisher and William Ury, *Getting to Yes: Negotiating Agreement Without Giving In*, Houghton Mifflin, 1981.

Rory Sutherland, *Alchemy: The Dark Art and Curious Science of Creating Magic in Brands*, Business and Life, HarperCollins, 2019.

Russ Roberts, *How Adam Smith Can Change Your Life: An Unexpected Guide to Human Nature and Happiness*, Penguin Books, 2015.

Ryan Holiday, *Ego Is the Enemy*, Portfolio/Penguin, 2016.

Seth Godin, *This Is Marketing: You Can't Be Seen Until You Learn to See*, Portfolio, 2018.

Shri Granth, Shri Anandpur Satsang Ashram (Trust).

Swami Prabhupada, *Bhagavad Gita As it Is*, The Bhaktivedanta Trust, 1968.

Tirthnath Mishra, Rumi's Masnavi: History and Indian Context.

Warren Buffett's Letters to Shareholders: 1967–2023, Berkshire Hathaway.

William Green, *Richer*, Wiser, Happier: How the World's Greatest Investors Win in Markets and Life, Scribner, 2021.

Acknowledgements

To Paramhans Dayalji, the founder of Shri Paramhans Advait Mat and Shri Anandpur Trust, my spiritual guru—for his grace in guiding me towards the broader purpose of life.

To Papaji, Tek Chand Chawla—a dedicated son, father, grandfather, both familial and societal, and most importantly, a good man. His children look up to him not merely with the naïve admiration of kids who believe their parent is the best, but with a deepening respect that has only grown stronger with each passing day. As they encountered the intricacies of the world, the familial learnings (sanskaar in Hindi) he instilled were continually reinforced.

To my mother, Bimla Chawla, for simply being herself—for giving my life purpose and direction by her very presence and unconditional love.

This book is for them together—for Mom and Dad. In Hindi: maa-baap, or Bimtek—an acronym formed from both their names, and fittingly the brand name of my investment office and business ventures.

To my sisters: for the love, affection, care towards their youngest sibling; and though I was younger, for allowing me to be the elder brother to them!

To my partner—for bearing with me each day, for her unconditional support, for helping me become a better man: gentler, kinder, more compassionate; and for creating the peace and tranquillity at home that have enabled me to step out and fight the supposed 'battles' in the world.

And finally, to my literary agent, Suhail Mathur, and Westland Books, for their faith and support in bringing this book together.